ROZ JACOBS

PAINTINGS AND PROCESS

ROZ JACOBS

PAINTINGS AND PROCESS

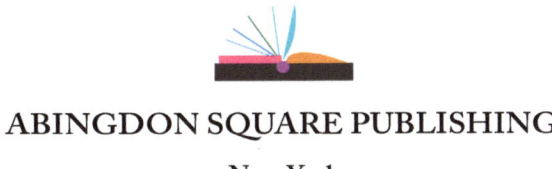

ABINGDON SQUARE PUBLISHING

New York

ROZ JACOBS
PAINTINGS & PROCESS
is published by
Abingdon Square Publishing Ltd.
463 West Street, Suite G122
New York, NY 10014 USA
www.abingdonsquarepublishing.com

Book Design: Abingdon Square Publishing
Cover Art: *Puycalvel Field* © Roz Jacobs, 2010

ISBN 978-0-9823480-9-3
Library of Congress Control Number: 2010939577

First Printing: November 2010
Printed in the United States of America

TABLE OF CONTENTS

Artist's Statement

Twenty years ago while travelling in southwestern France, I was mesmerized by the sight of an old man with a scythe clearing a field at sunset. I knew that this landscape and way of life would disappear within my lifetime—but it was still a bridge to the past. A few years later I bought and renovated a centuries old stone barn in the same part of rural France. Though born and based in New York City, I've returned to the same landscape year after year since then. I try to capture in paint the things that don't change—the spirit of the place, the light, the movement of the wind.

I often paint outdoors in the moonlight. With moonlight vision there is little room for revision. There is an urgency to capture the night scene in one "take." The pigments are always in the same position on my palette, so my brush knows where to go as my eye is on the scene before me. It is a swift and intense engagement and when I re-enter my studio and see what I have done it is always a surprise.

While I paint most of my landscapes and moon paintings *en plein air,* I also work from memory in my studio. There, I recall the traces of the painting process that are hidden beneath the surface of the artwork. I ask myself how can I bring viewers into the time capsule of my painting's memory?

In some paintings I divide a single canvas into a grid and the sections represent different stages of the process. In one section, I might keep the abstract moment of orienting myself in space with line and tone. In another, I might leave the musical

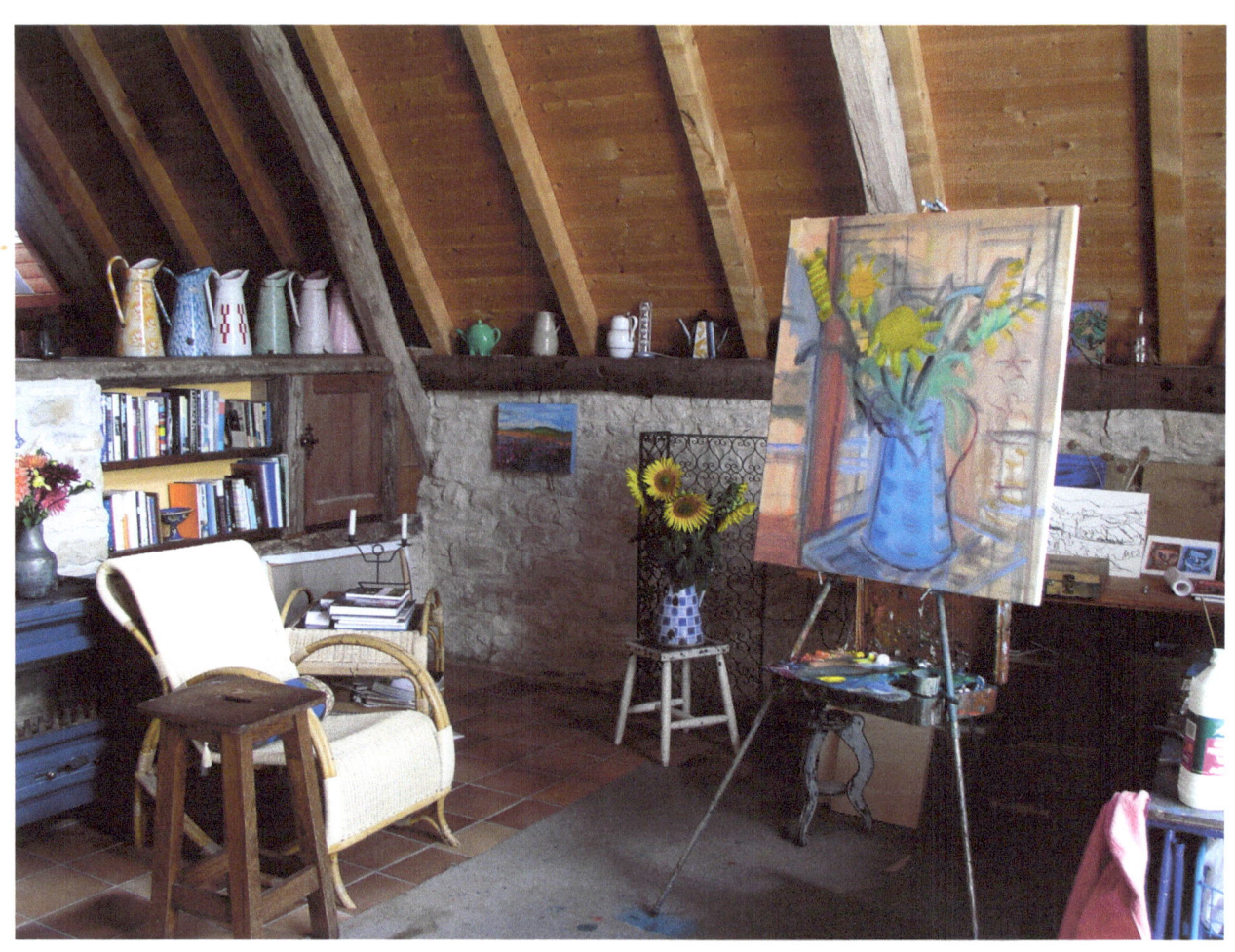

movements of the line moving toward and away as I'm navigating the third dimension and the flat picture plane. In another section, shapes in space or the interplay of light planes and geometric forms might be present.

In another approach to time and memory, I use videotape to show the painting process—capturing on tape, the compositions that are destroyed or recovered as a canvas evolves. This began with *The Memory Project,* a very personal project related to my family's history. I videotaped myself painting portraits of my mother's younger brother, a child who disappeared during the Holocaust. I captured on videotape the process of evoking in paint the memory of someone I knew only through my mother's stories and from a small photograph that she recovered after the war. I felt that I came to know my uncle as I studied that photograph and painted him over and over again, feeling his gesture of looking up at the photographer and connecting to him in that moment. It is to connect that I paint—to capture the eternal in the present.

My teacher, Norman Raeben, used to say "Art telescopes time." The past and the future are in the present moment that art is created. It's all contained in the painting.

— Roz Jacobs
New York, 2010

Sunflowers in Puycalvel (detail)

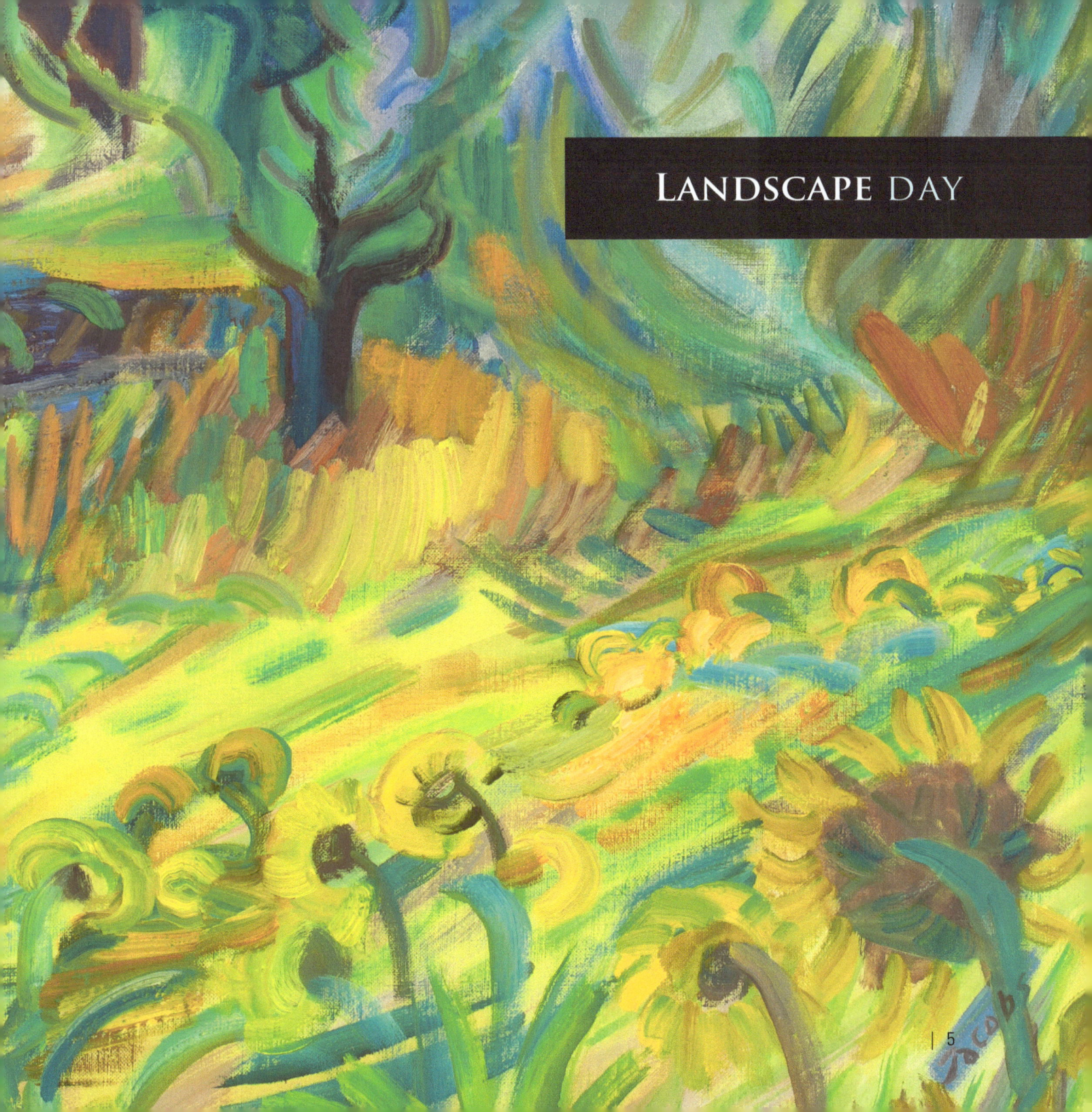

Puycalvel Field

Oil on linen, 30 x 34 inches

2010

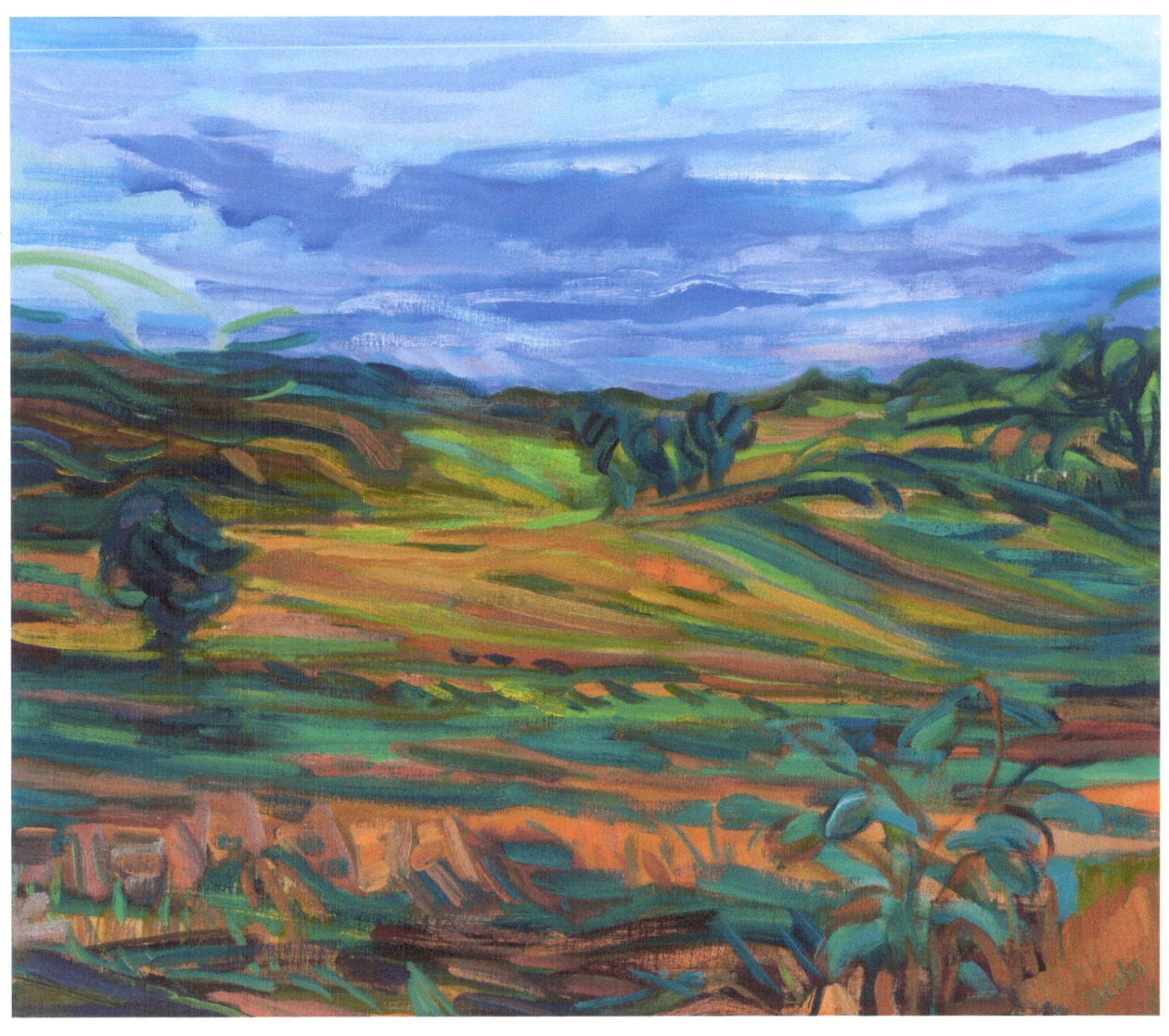

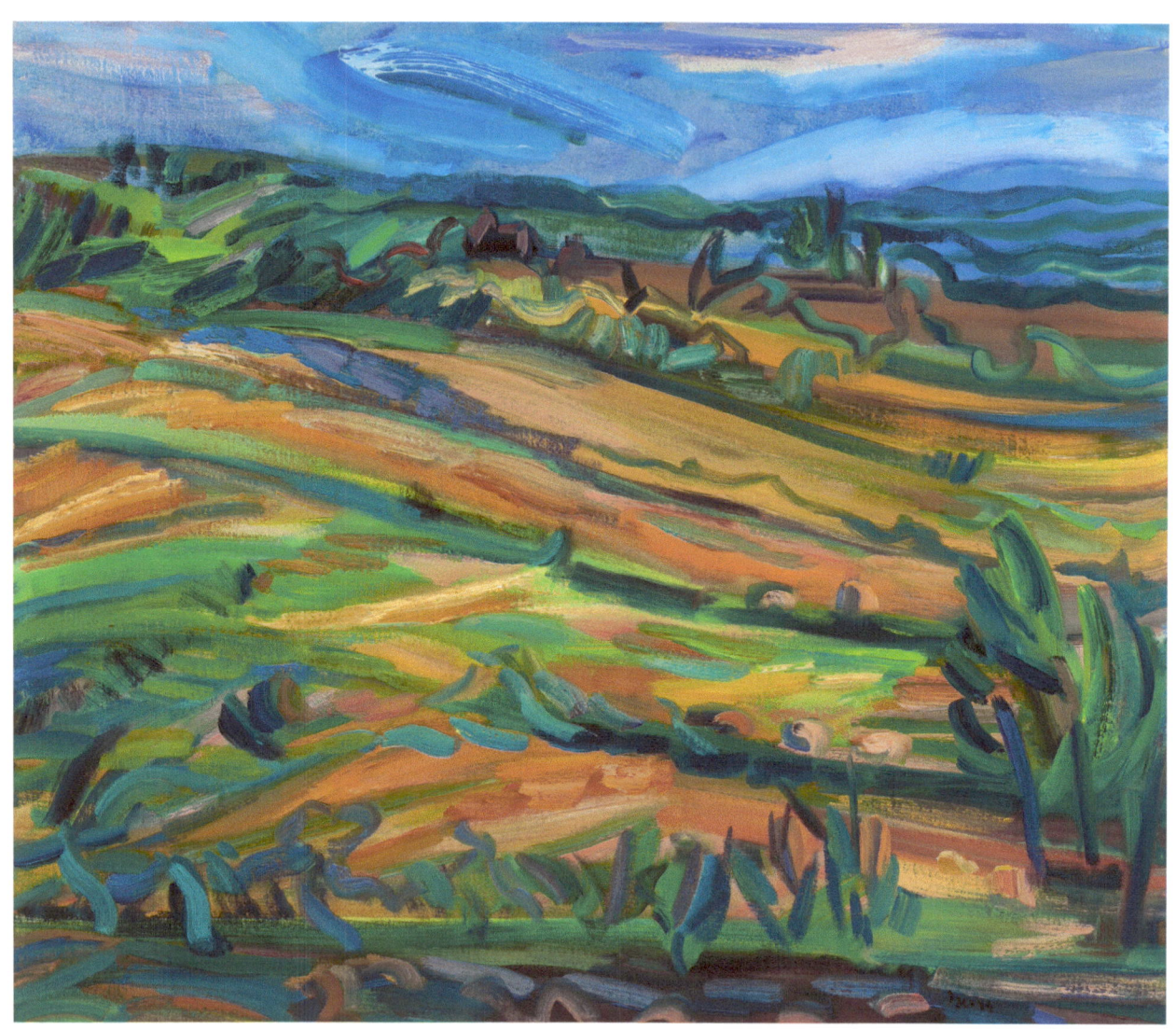

Puycalvel Fields

Oil on linen, 30 x 34 inches

2007

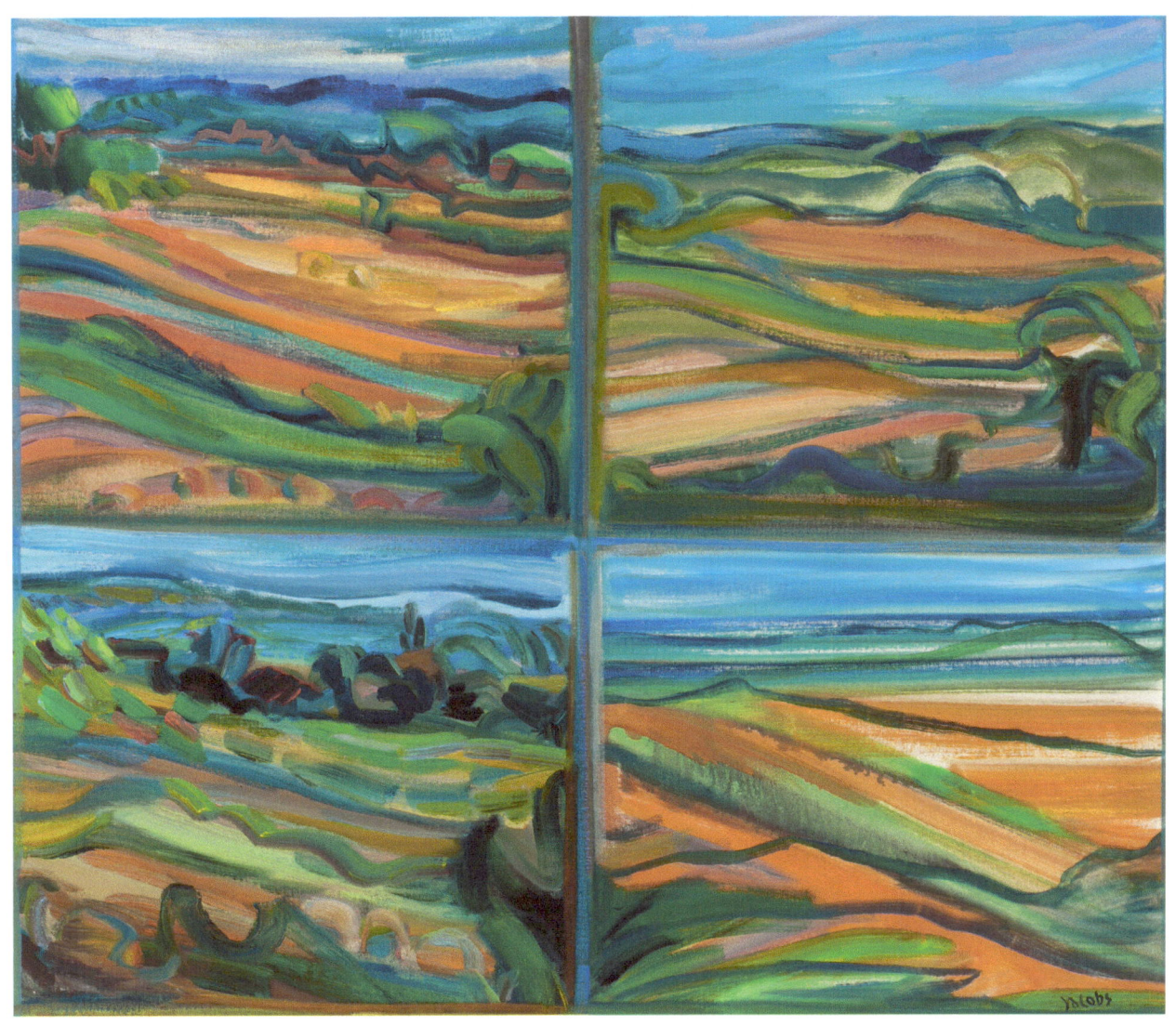

Puycalvel Fields Grid

Oil on linen, 30 x 34 inches

2007

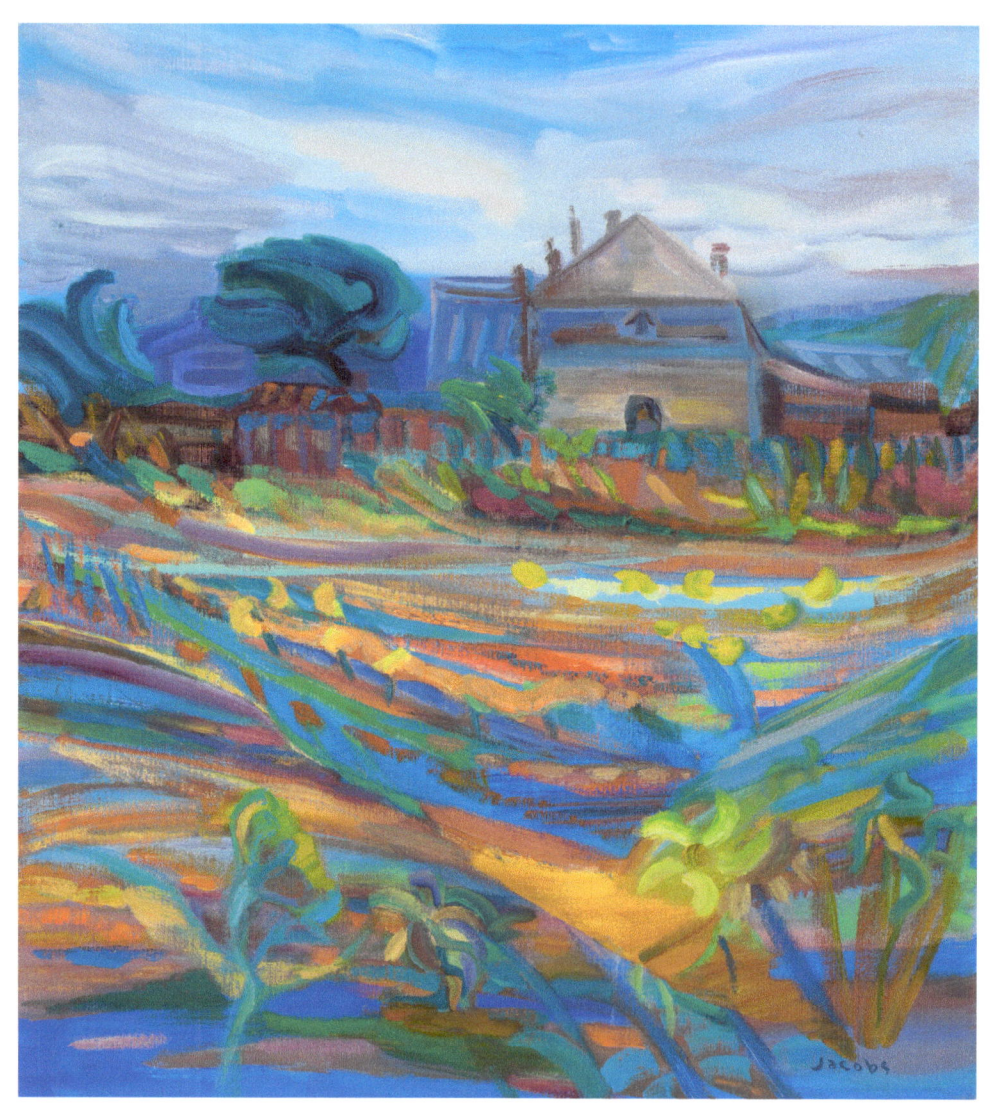

Loire Wildflowers

Oil on linen, 34 x 30 inches

2007

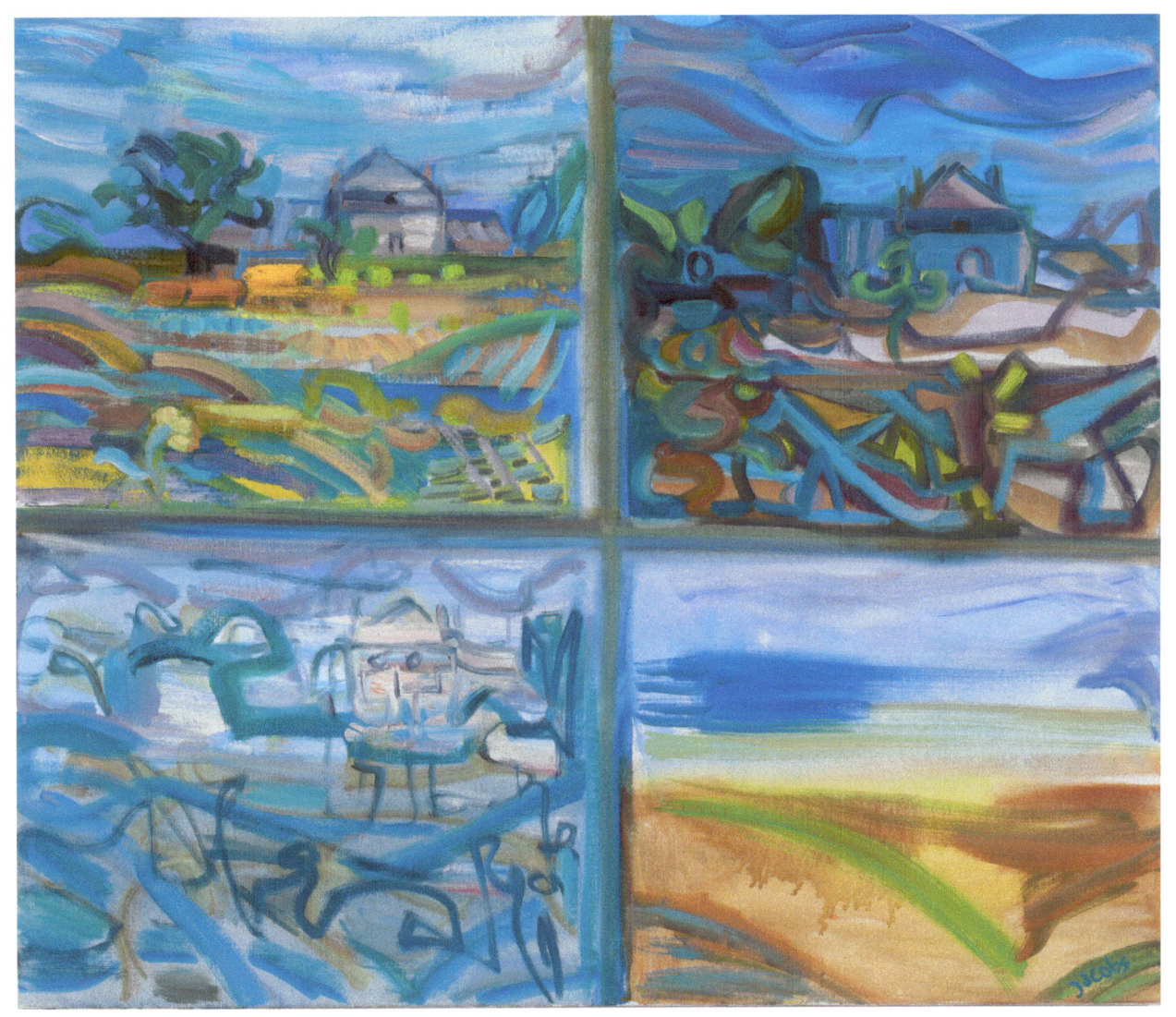

Loire Wildflowers Grid

Oil on linen, 30 x 34 inches

2007

Loire Wildflowers 2

Oil on linen, 22 x 30 inches

2006

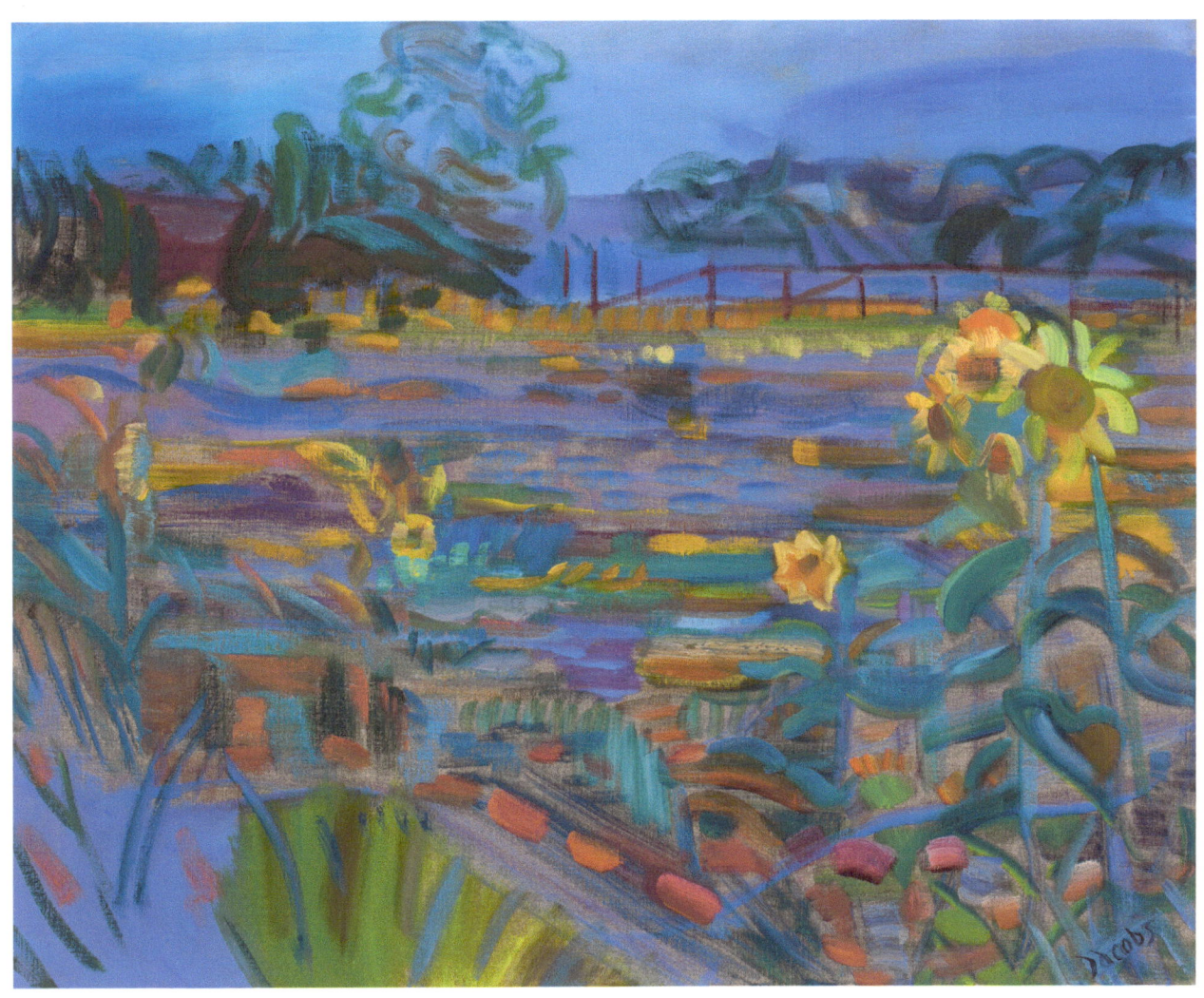

Loire Wildflowers 3

Oil on linen, 25 x 30 inches

2006

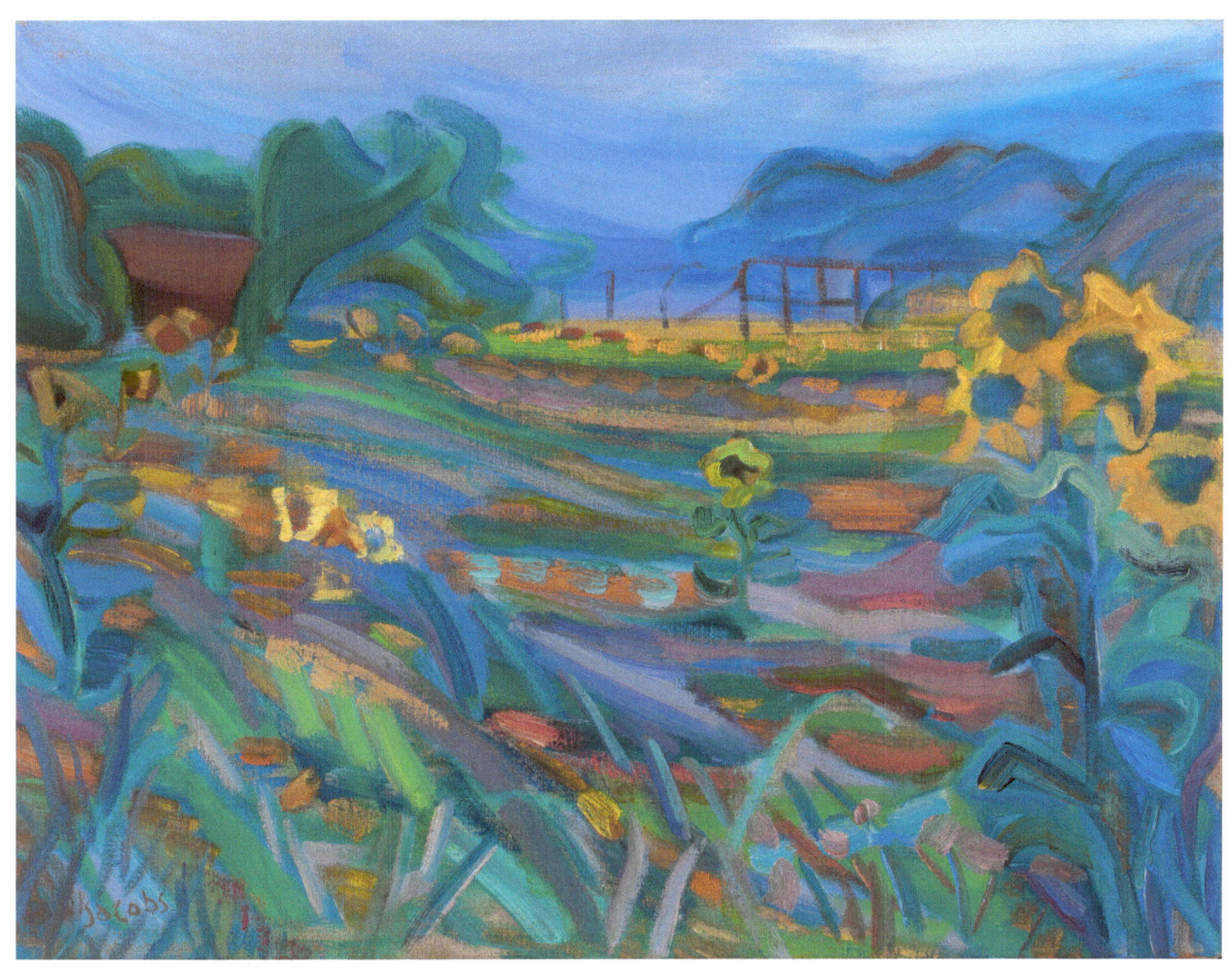

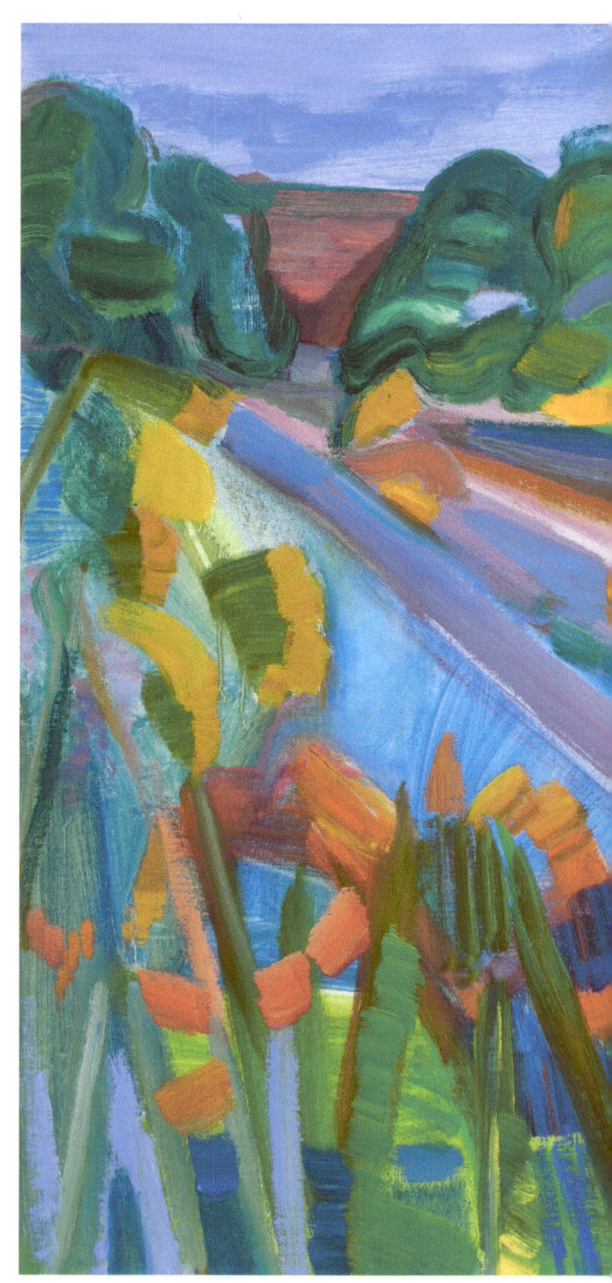

Loire Sunflowers

Oil on linen, 24 x 40 inches

2006

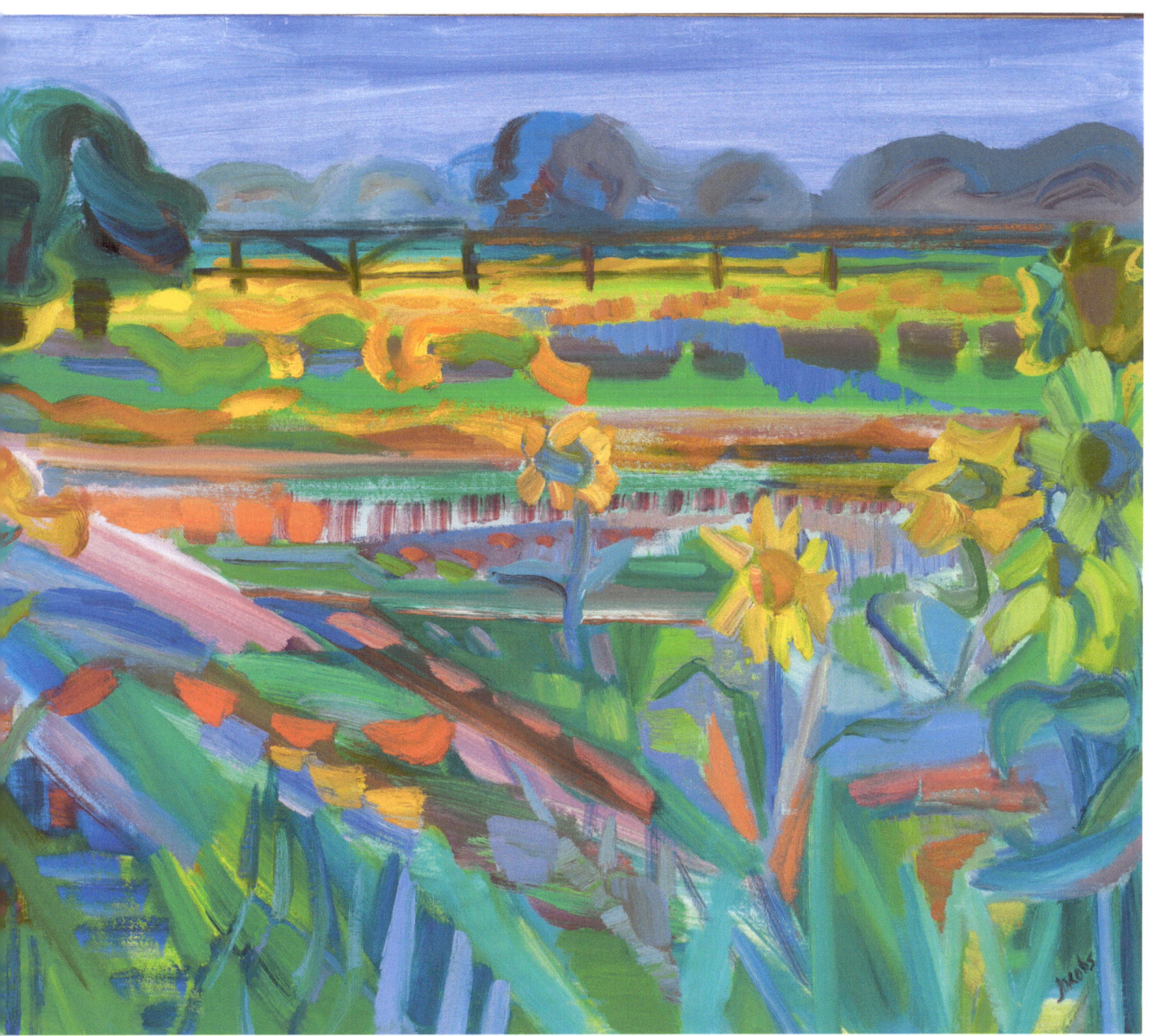

Sunflowers in Puycalvel

Oil on linen, 30 x 34 inches

2010

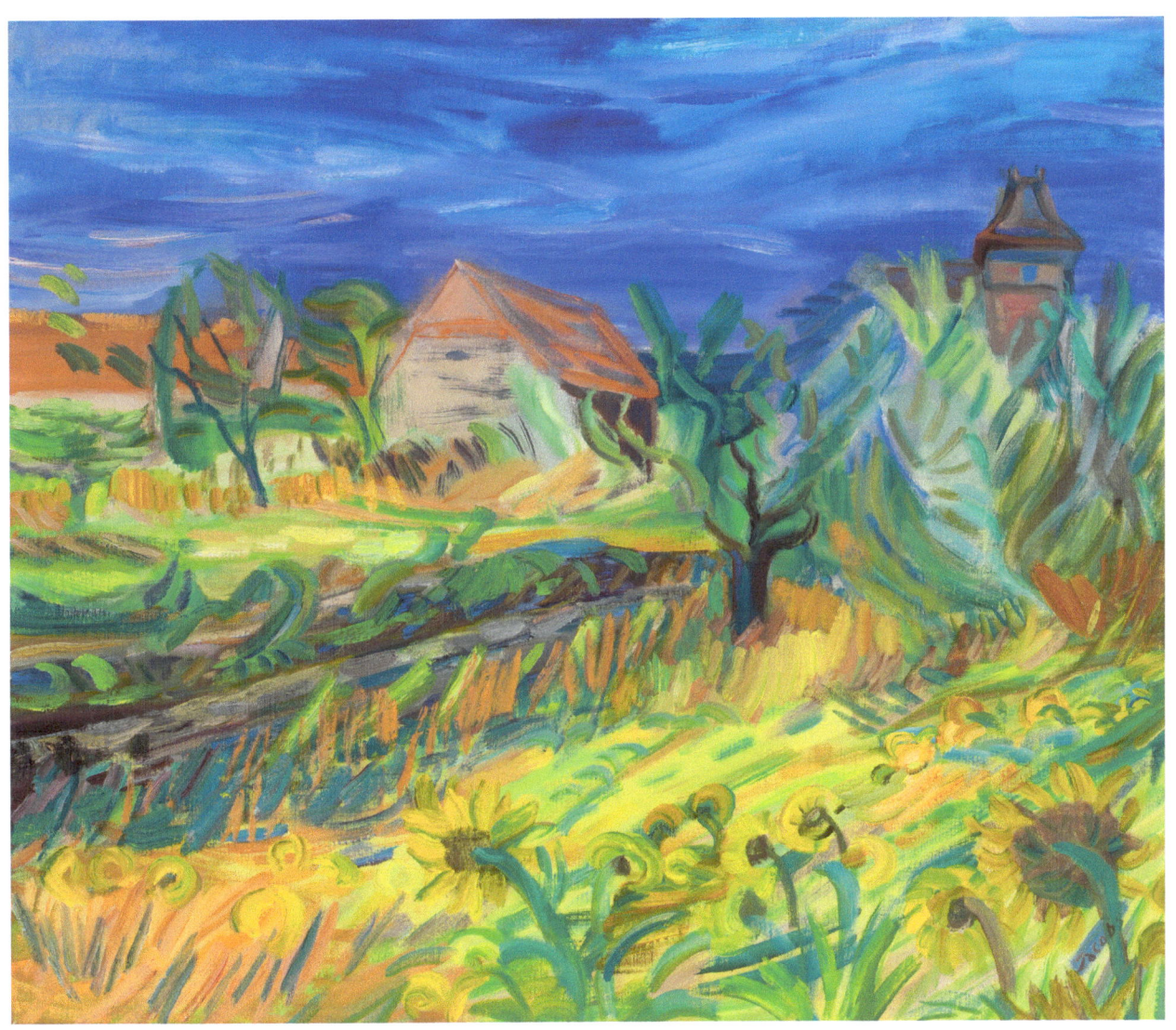

Lavacantiere

Oil on linen, 30 x 34 inches

2000

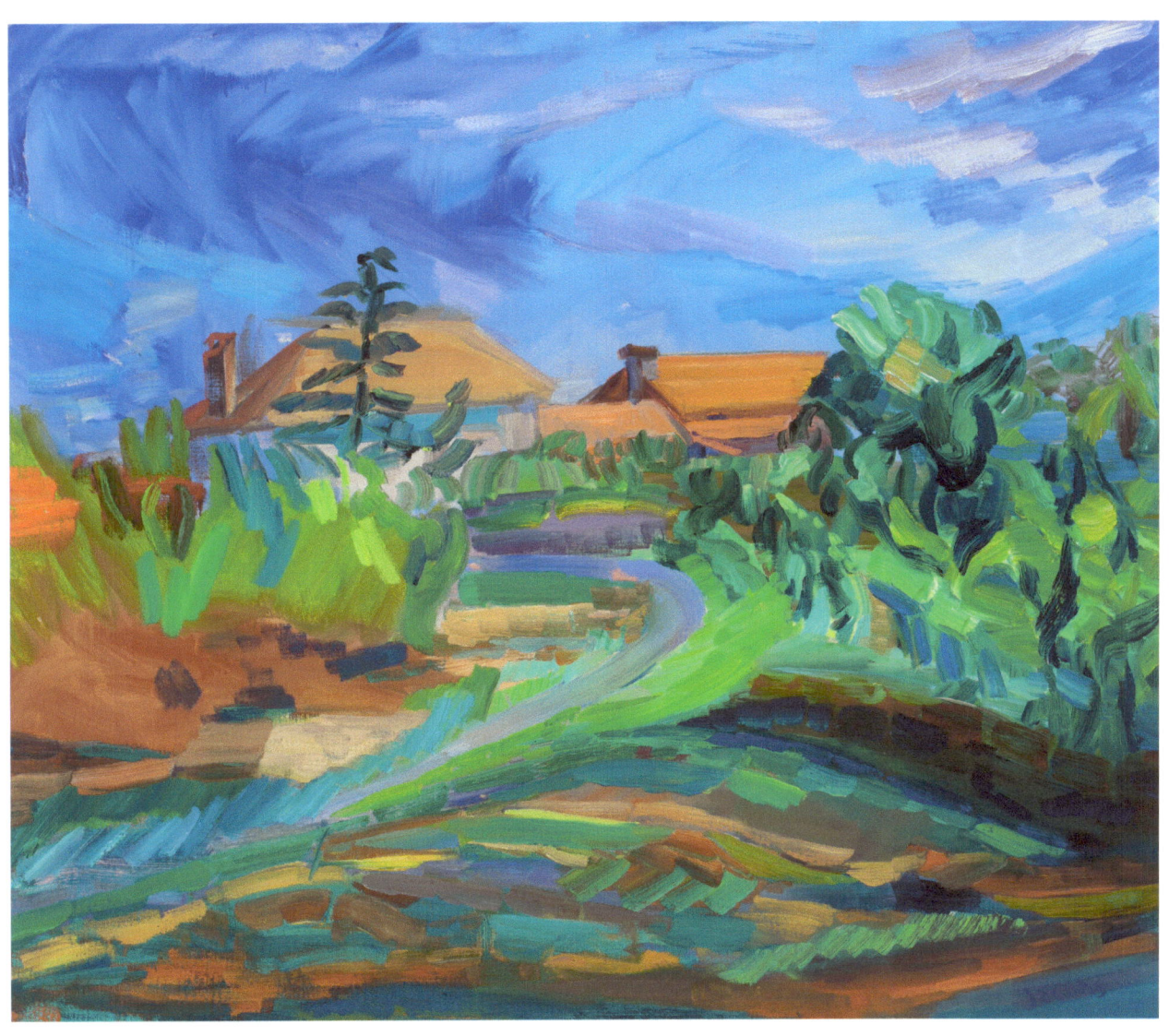

Aisha in the Afternoon

Oil on linen, 30 x 34 inches

2004

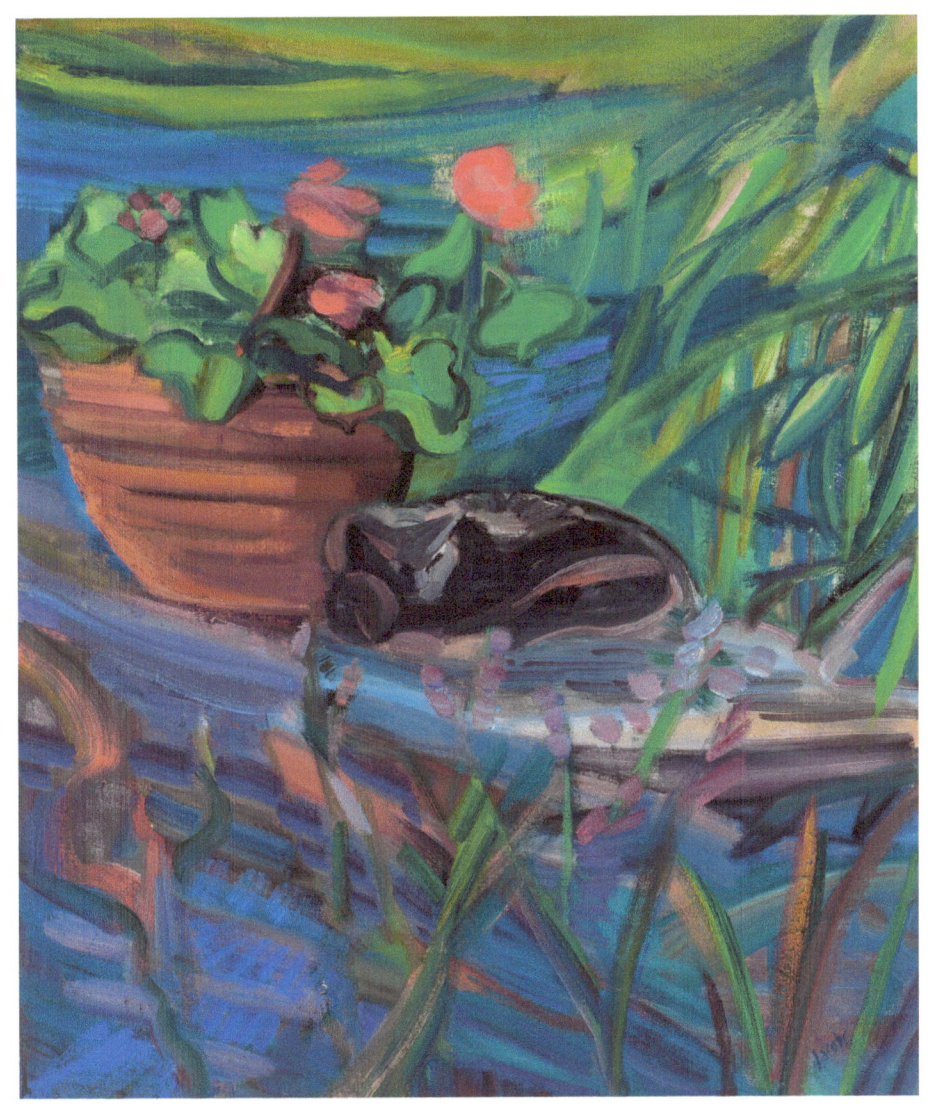

Pyrenées Landscape

Oil on linen, 25 x 32 inches

2003

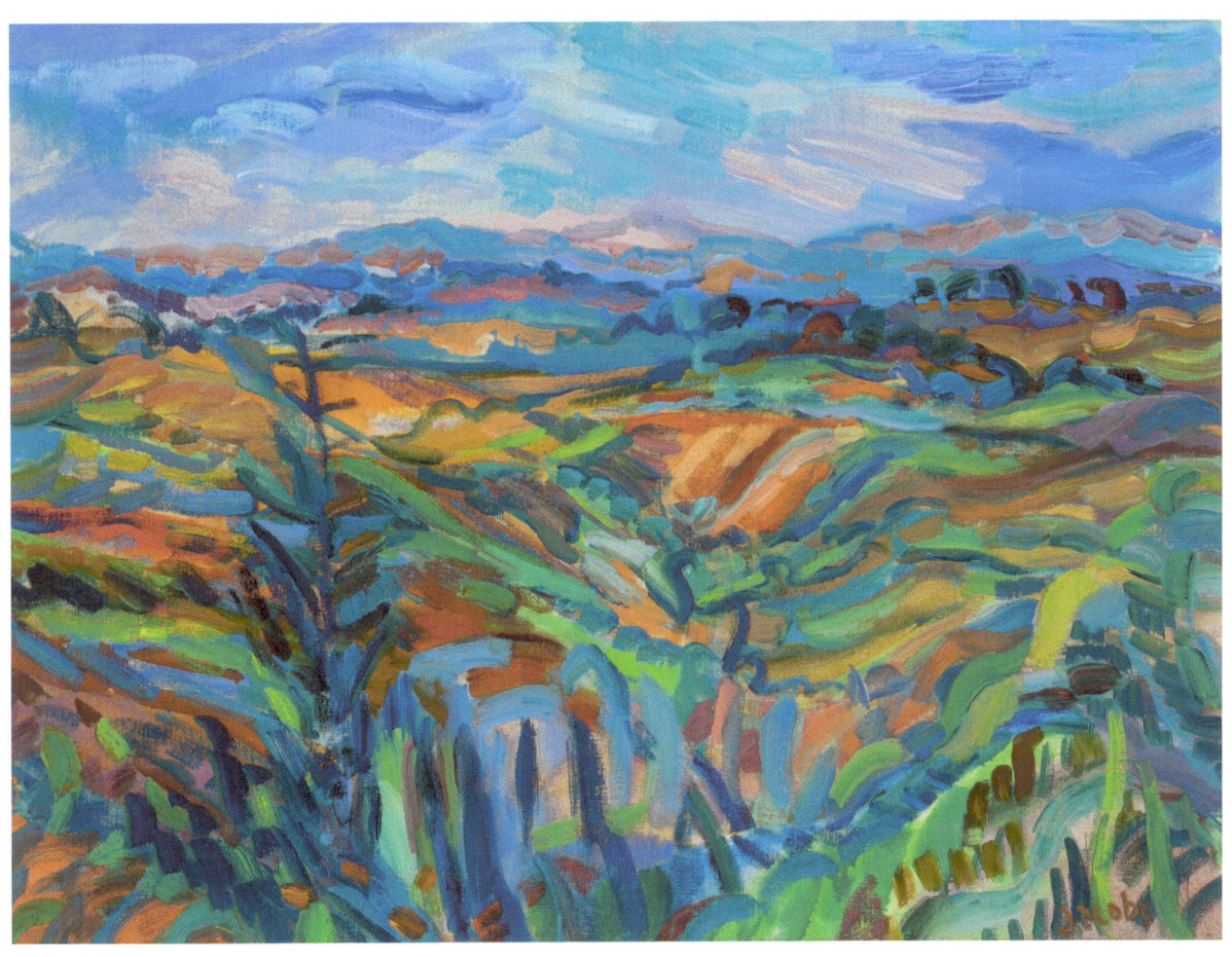

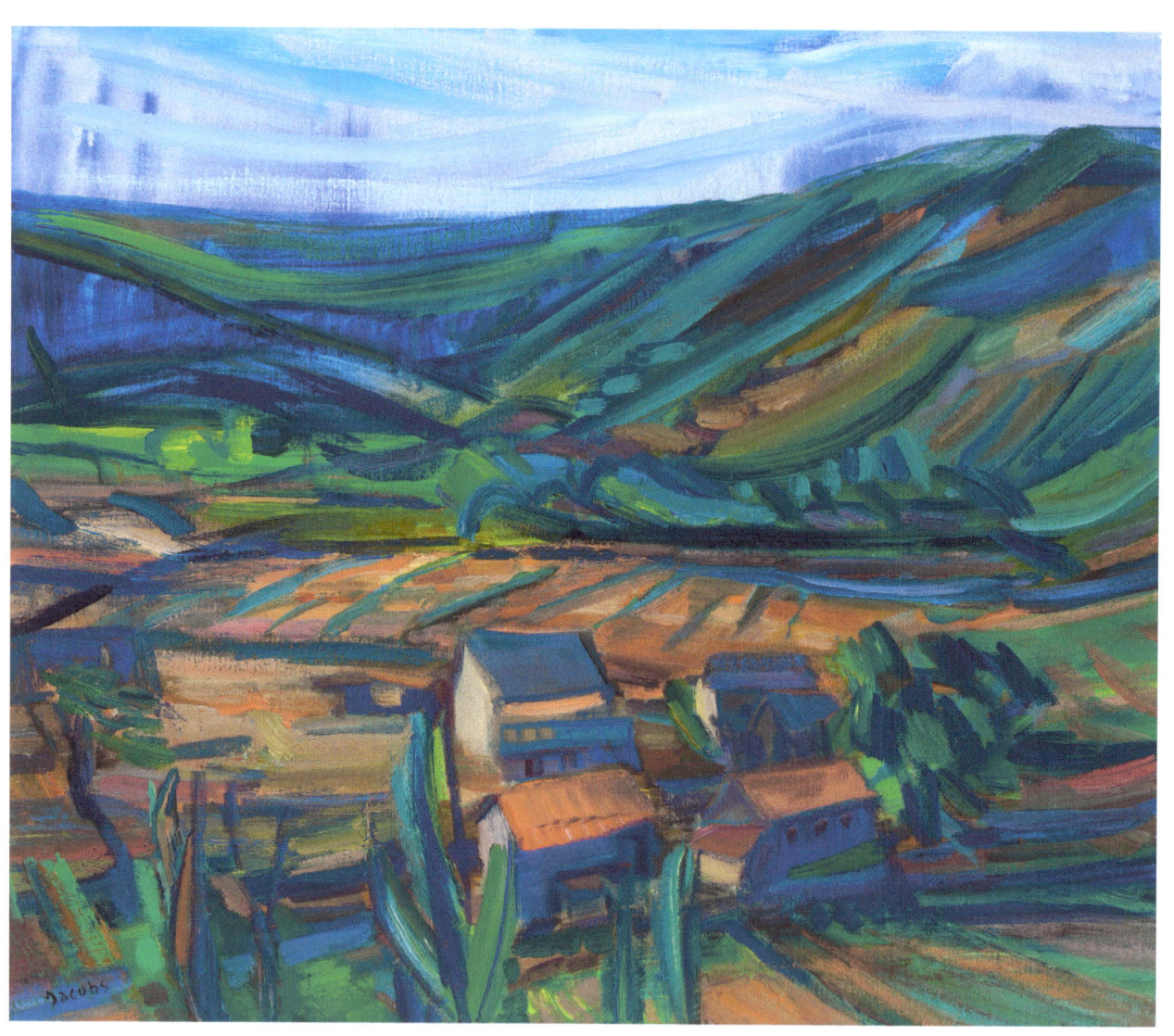

Lot Valley 2

Oil on linen, 30 x 34 inches

2003

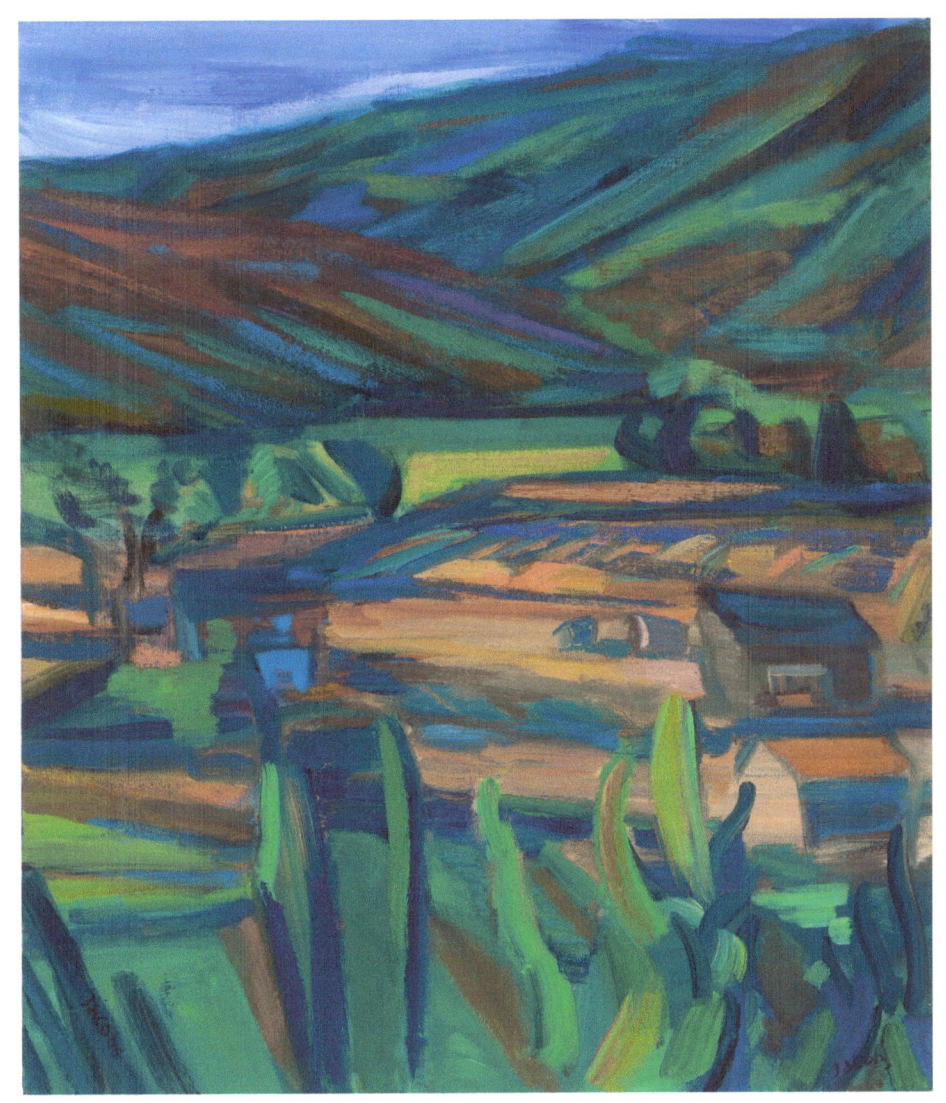

Lot Valley 3

Oil on linen, 30 x 25 inches

2003

Moonlit View (detail)

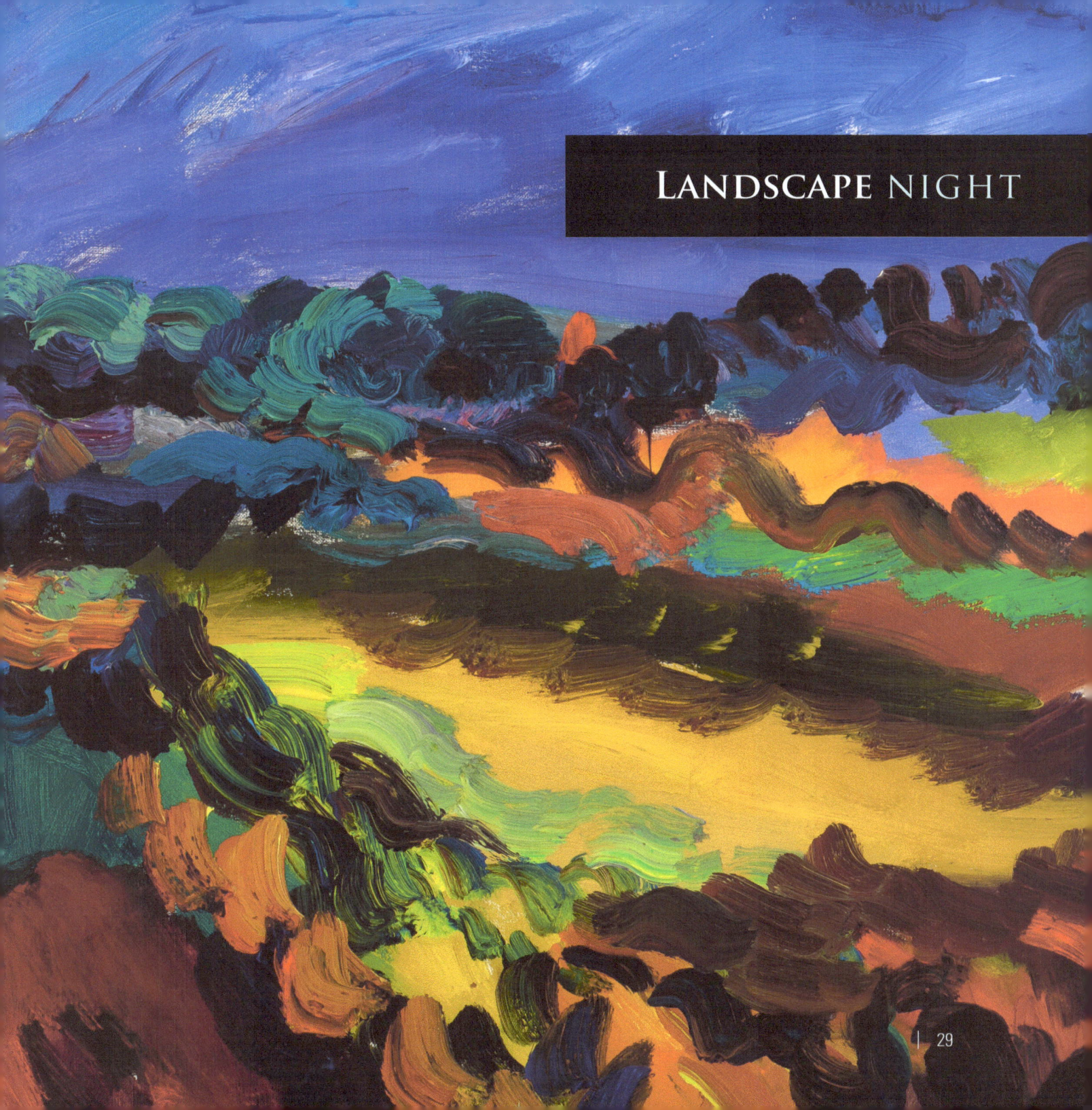

LANDSCAPE NIGHT

Moonrise in Puycalvel

Oil on linen, 25 x 30 inches

2009

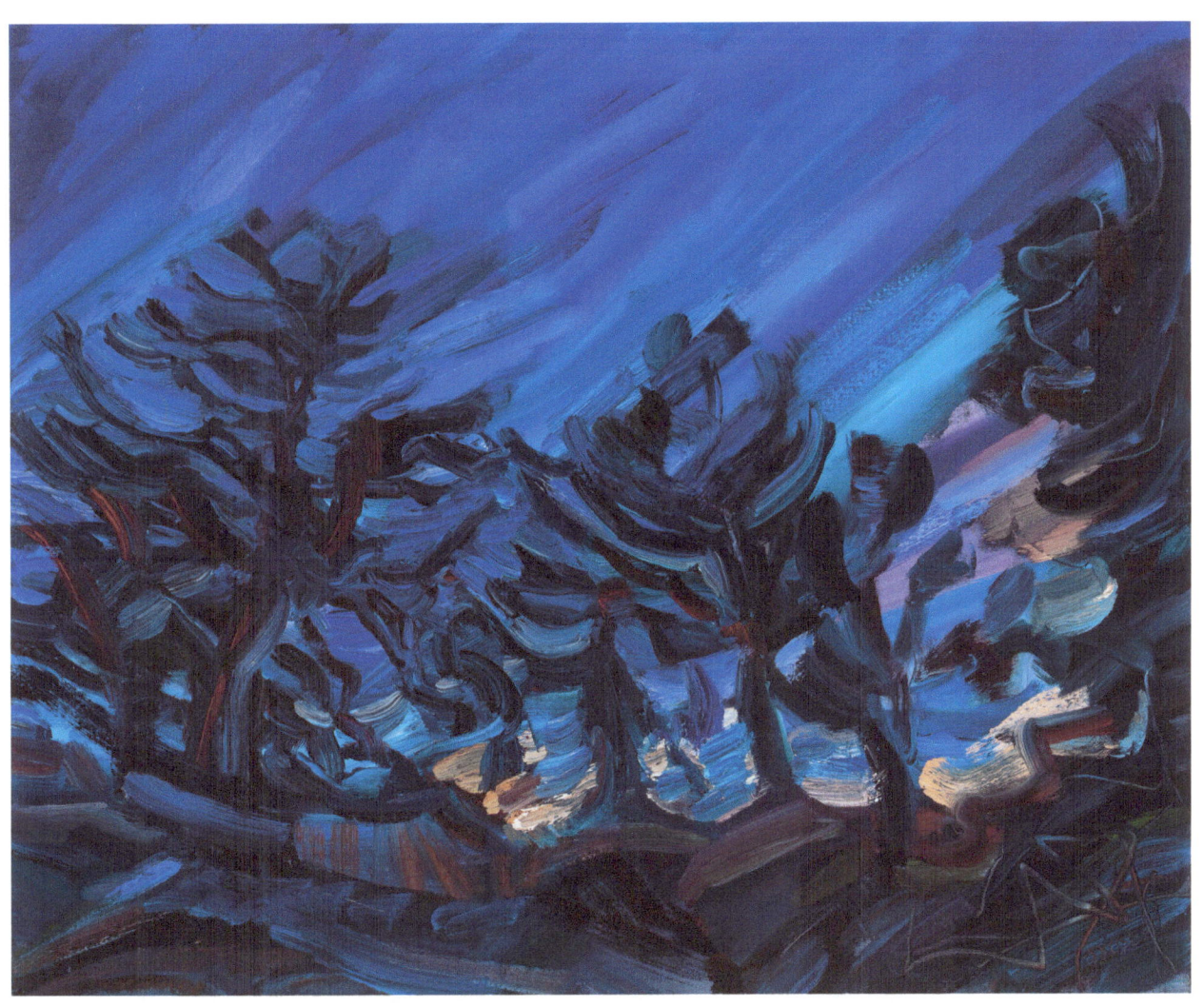

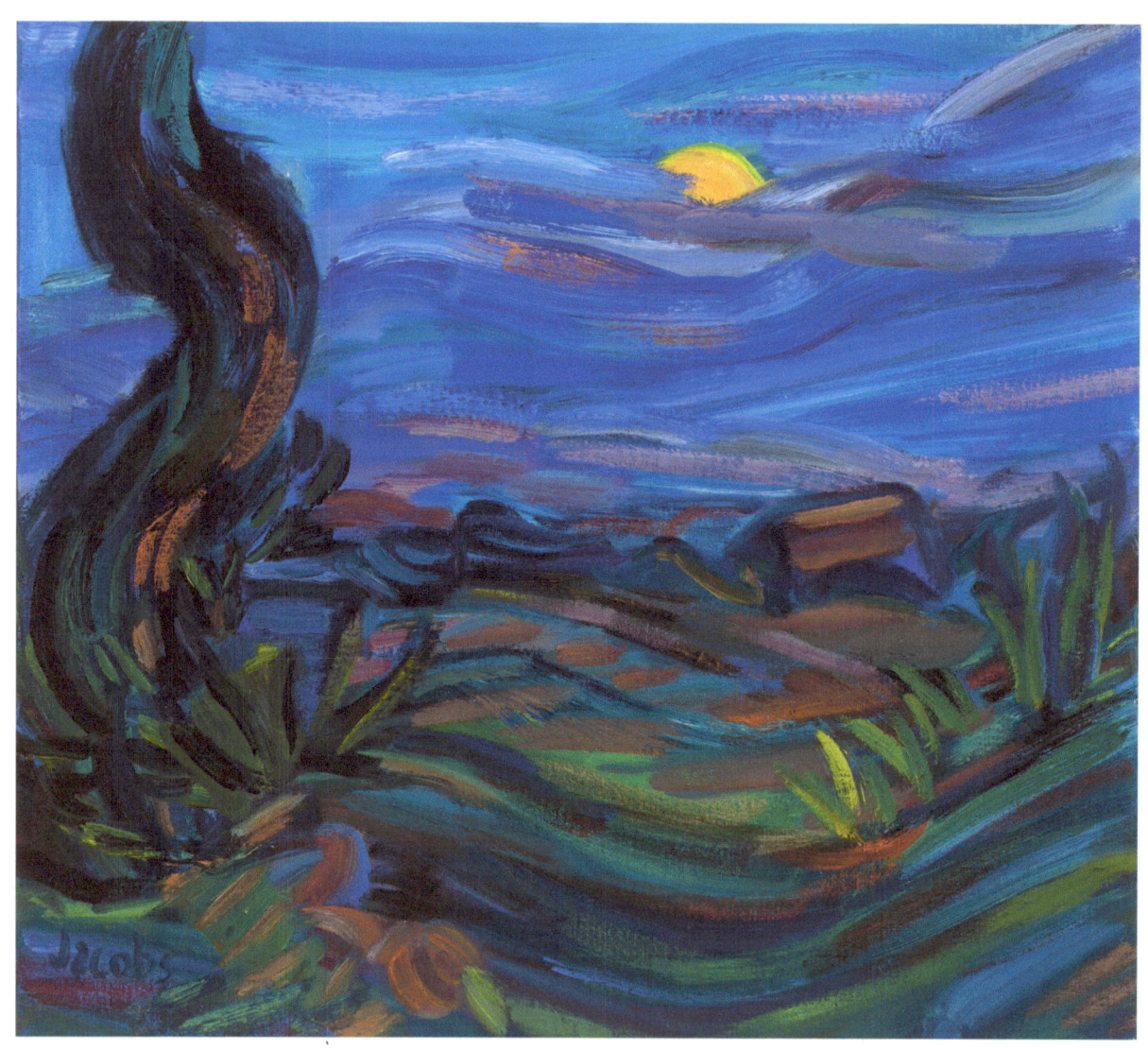

Cypress Moon

Oil on linen, 24 x 26 inches

2008

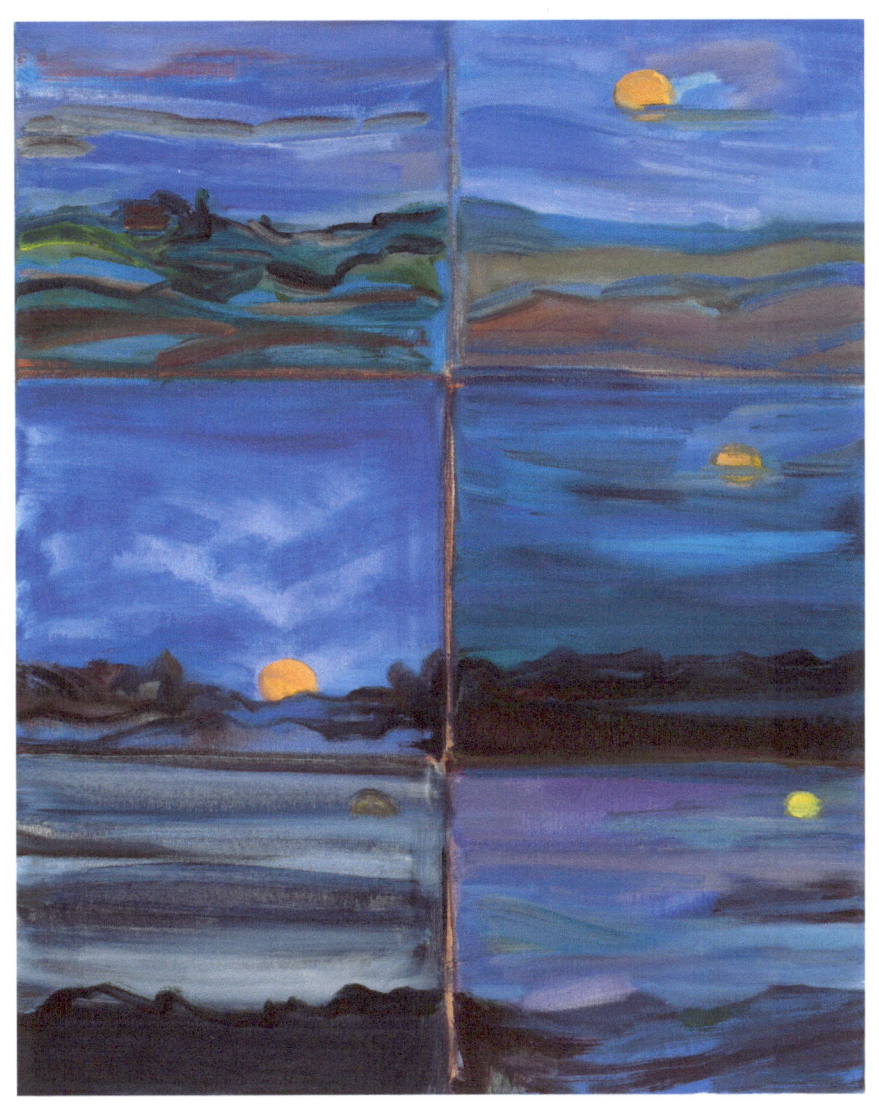

Moonrise Sextet

Oil on linen, 36 x 28 inches

2009

Moonrise 3

Oil on linen, 30 x 34 inches

2010

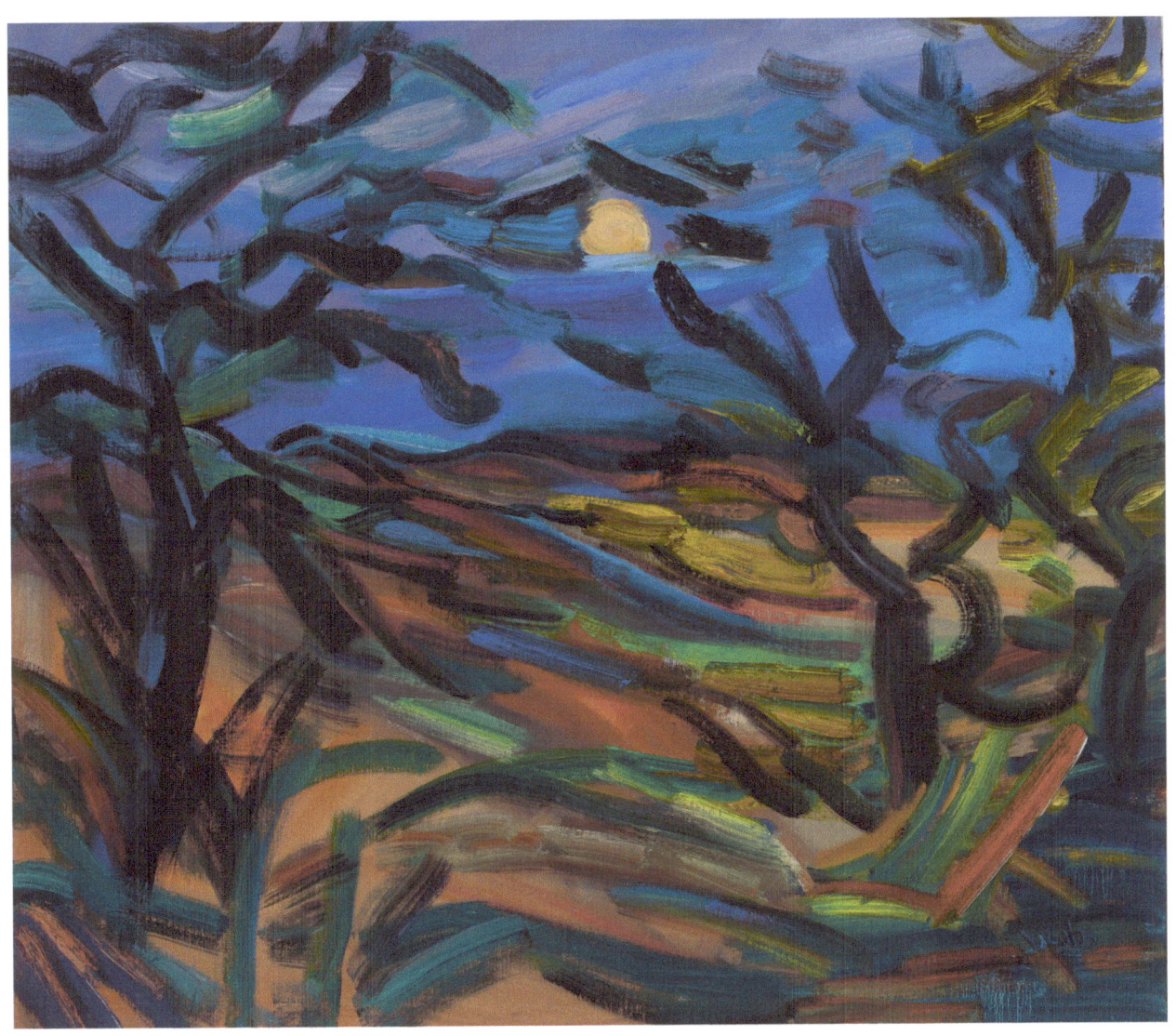

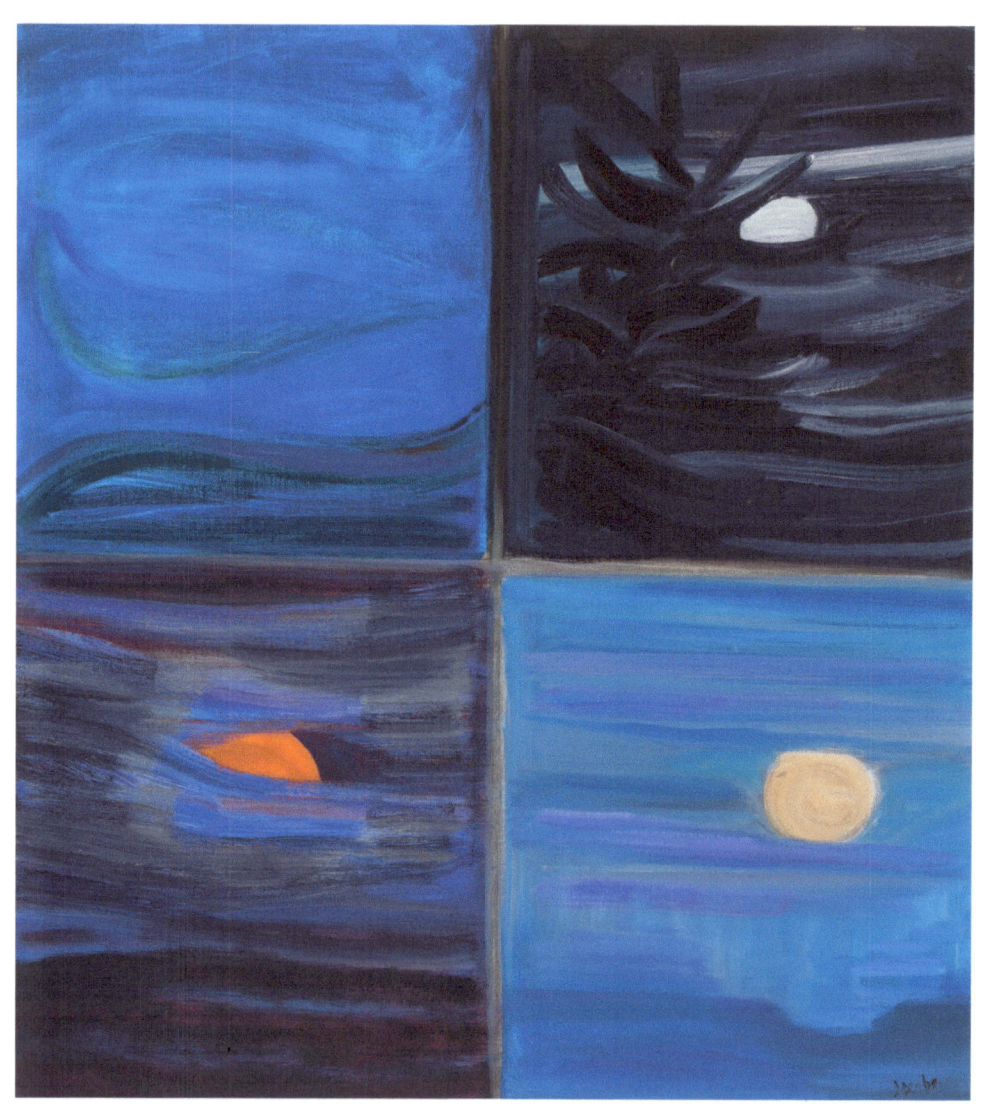

Moonlight Quartet 1

Oil on linen, 34 x 30 inches

2009

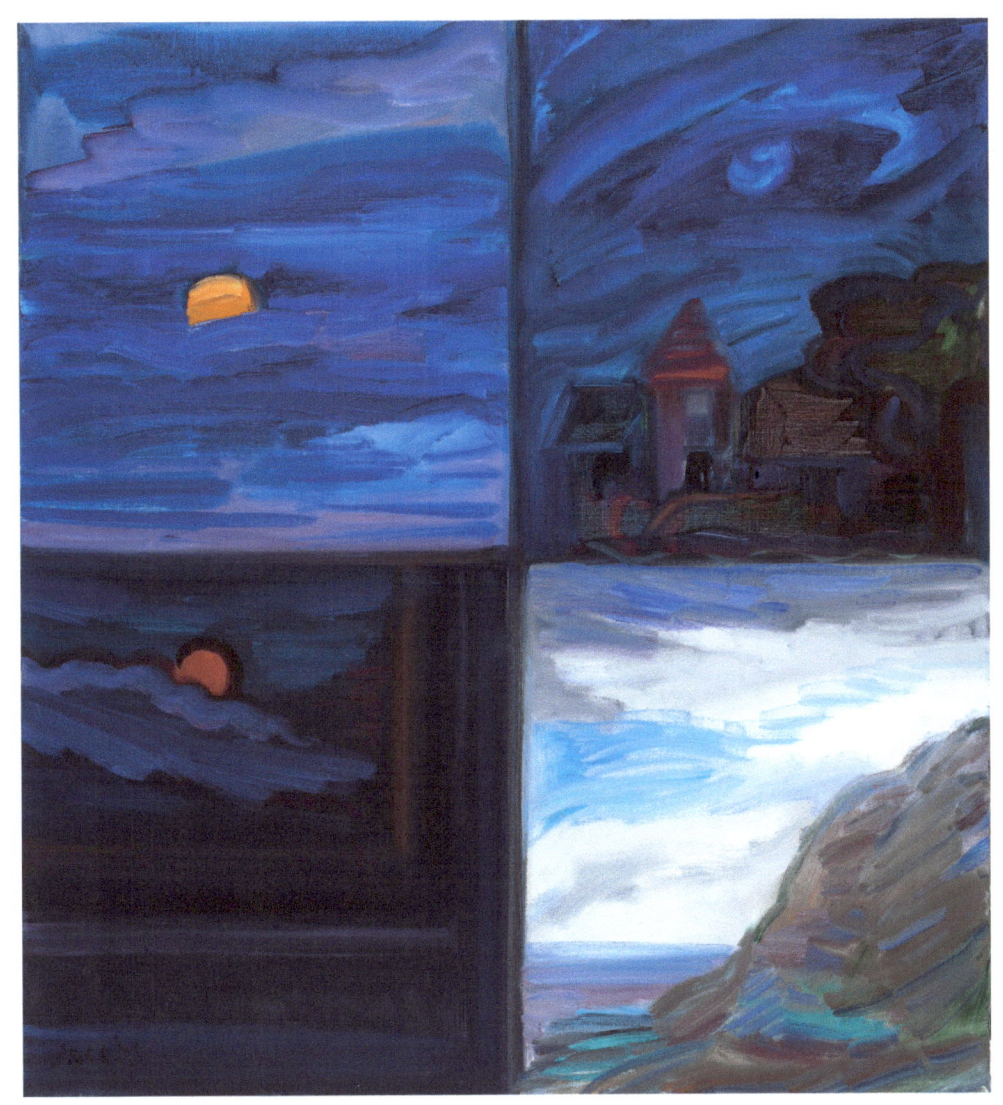

Moonlight Quartet 2

Oil on linen, 34 x 30 inches

2009

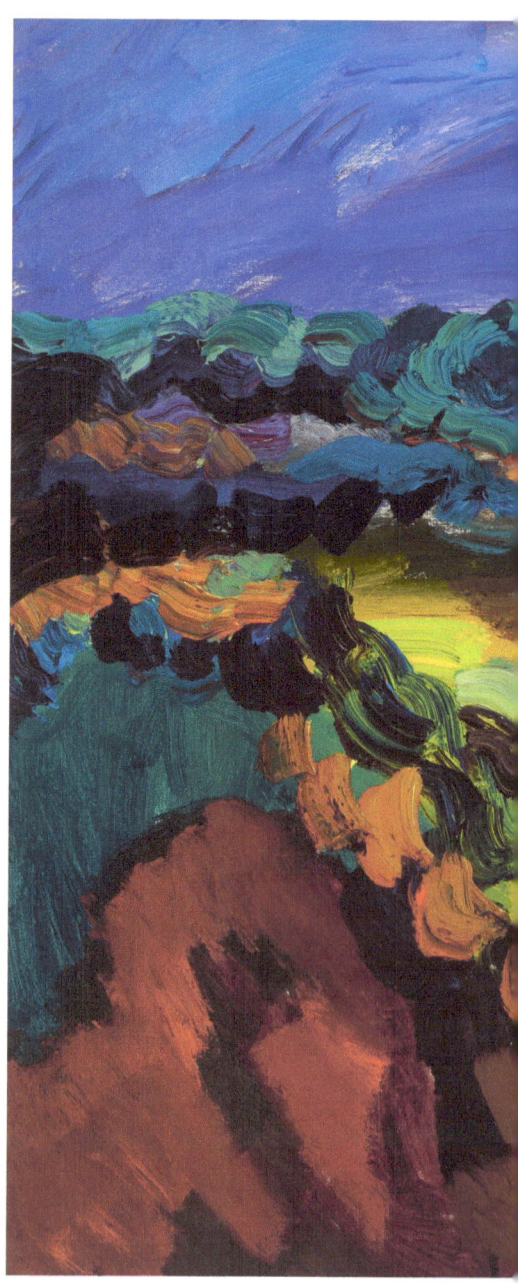

Moonlit View

Oil on linen, 25 x 40 inches

2001

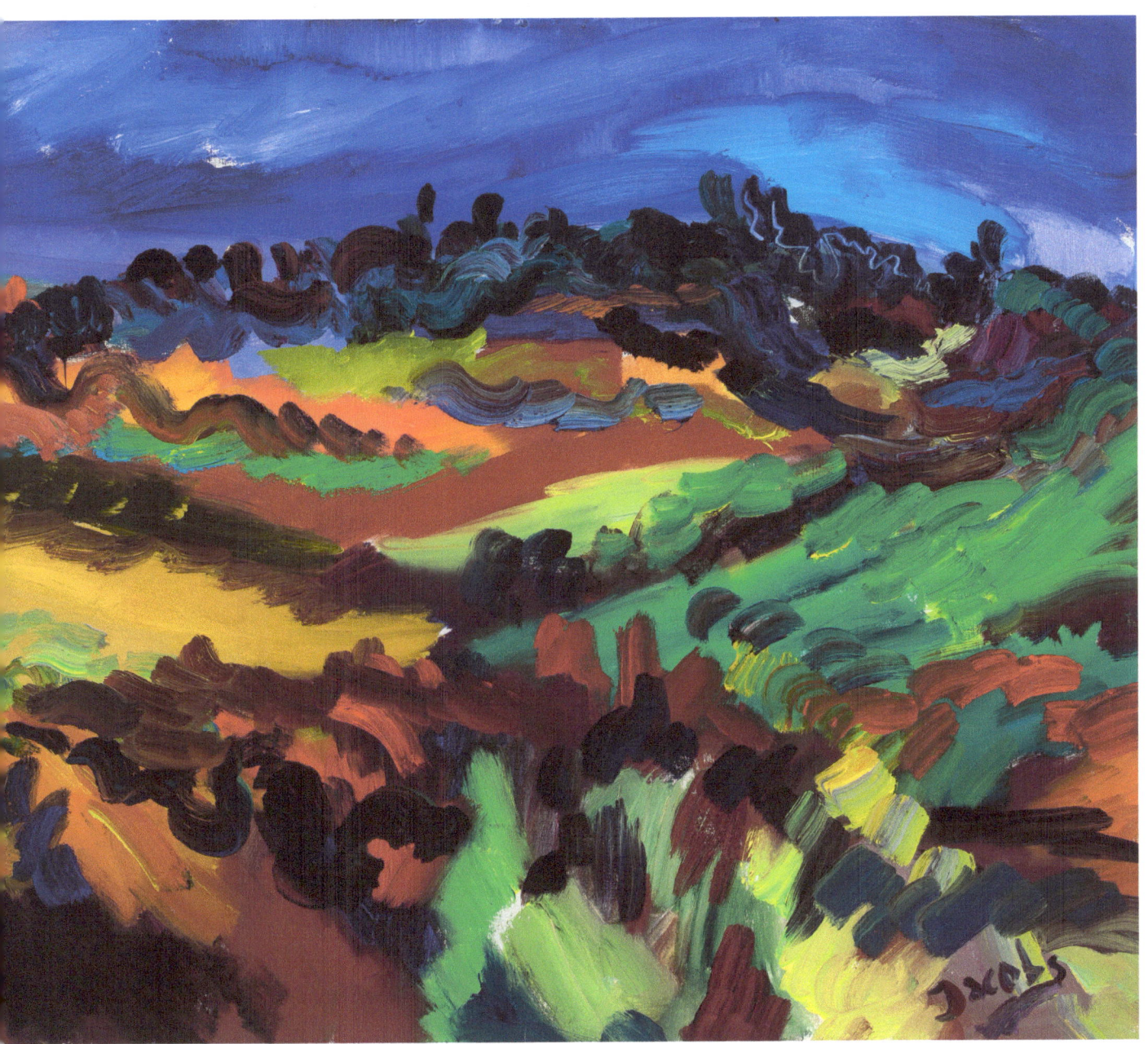

Moonrise 2

Oil on linen, 30 x 34 inches

2009

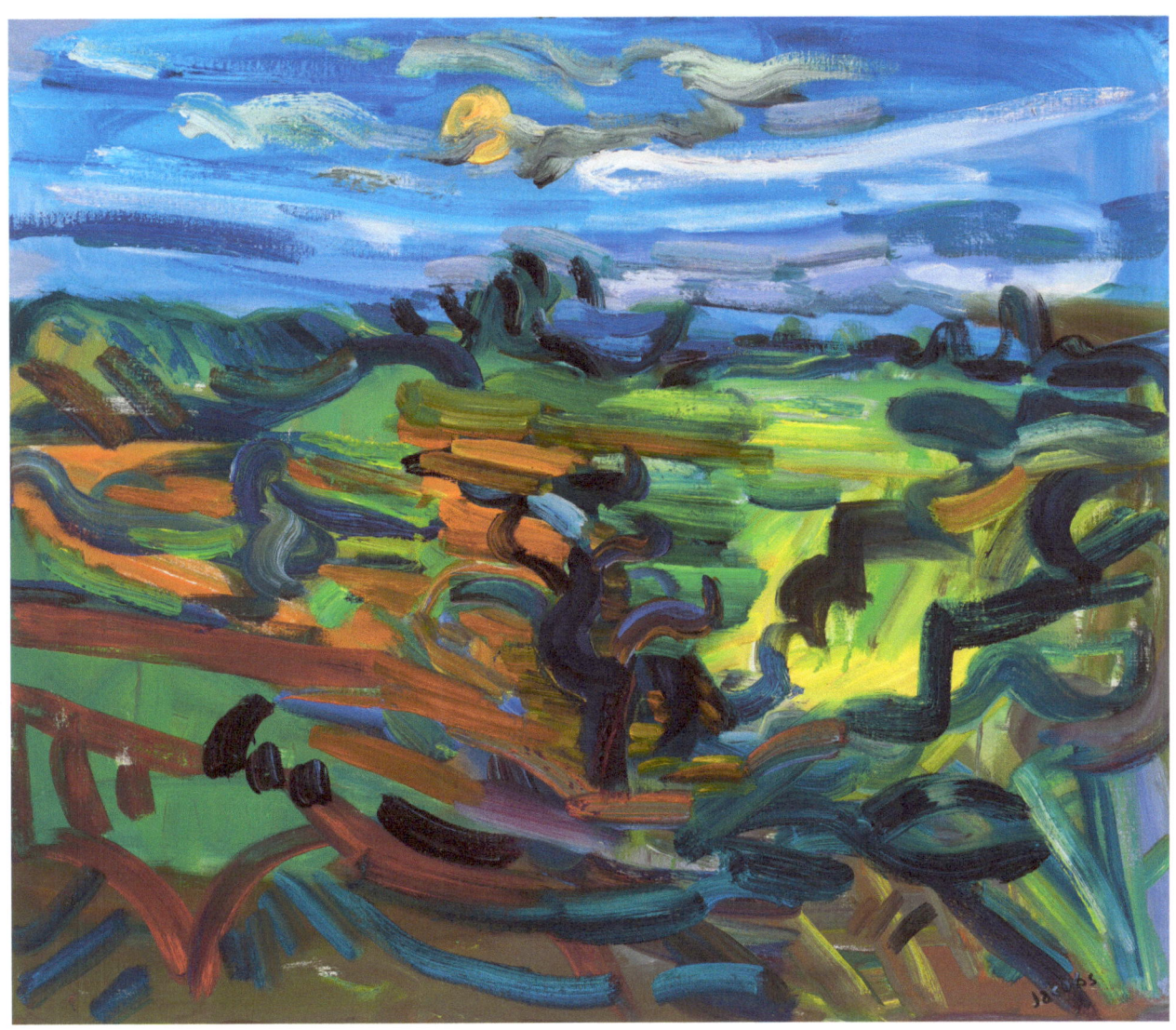

Moonlit Landscape

Oil on linen, 30 x 34 inches

2009

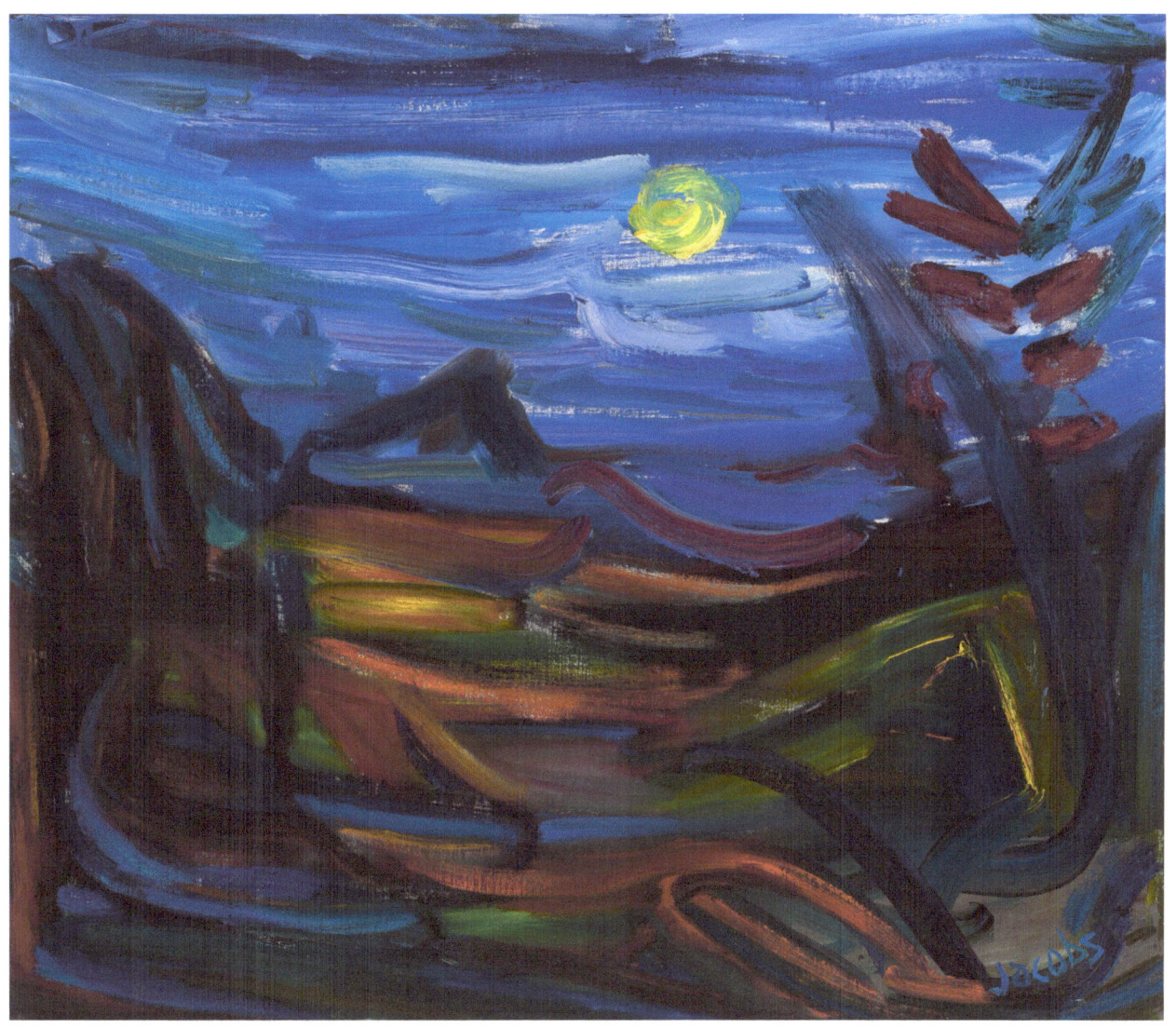

Day for Night

Oil on linen, 25 x 30 inches

2008

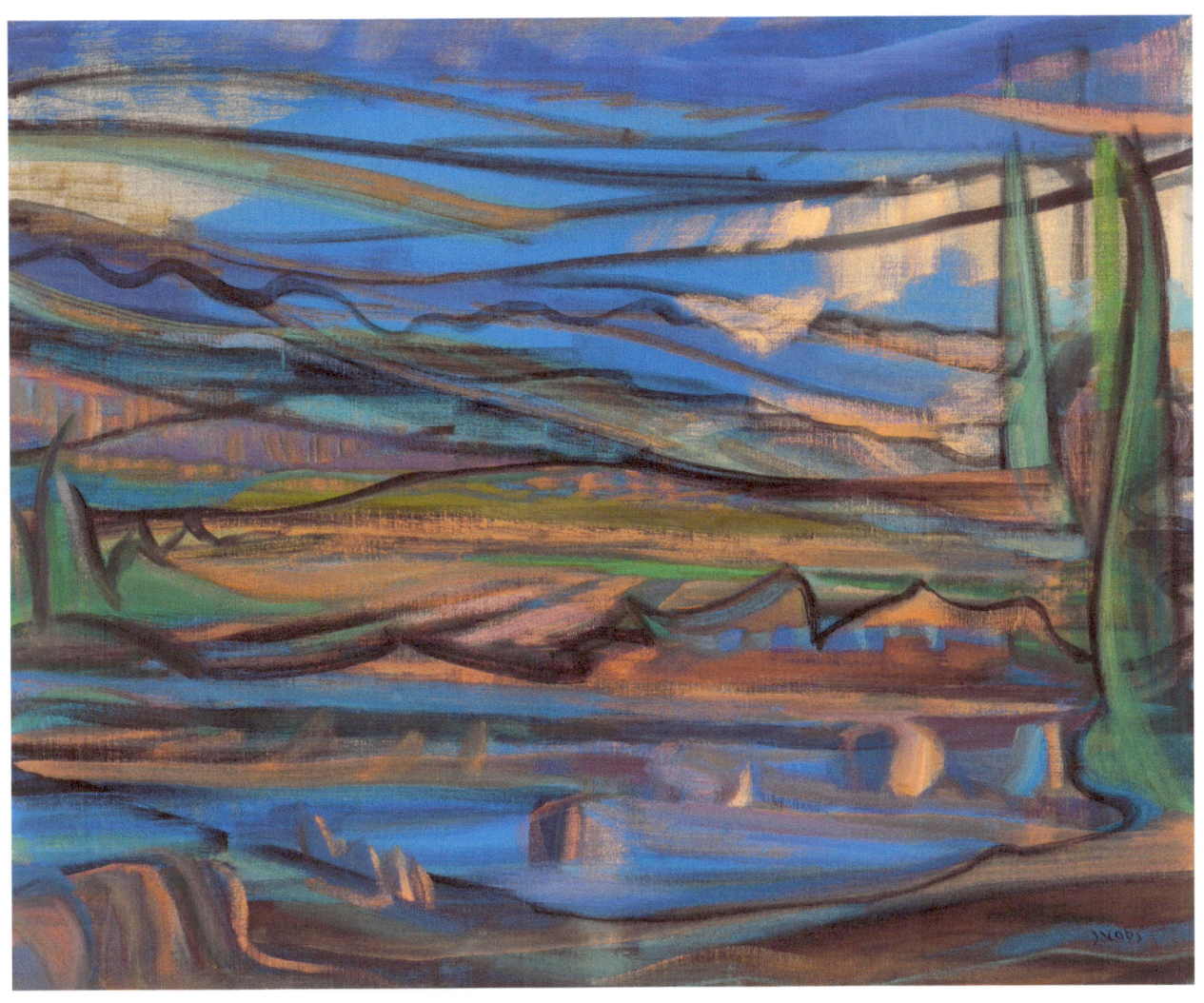

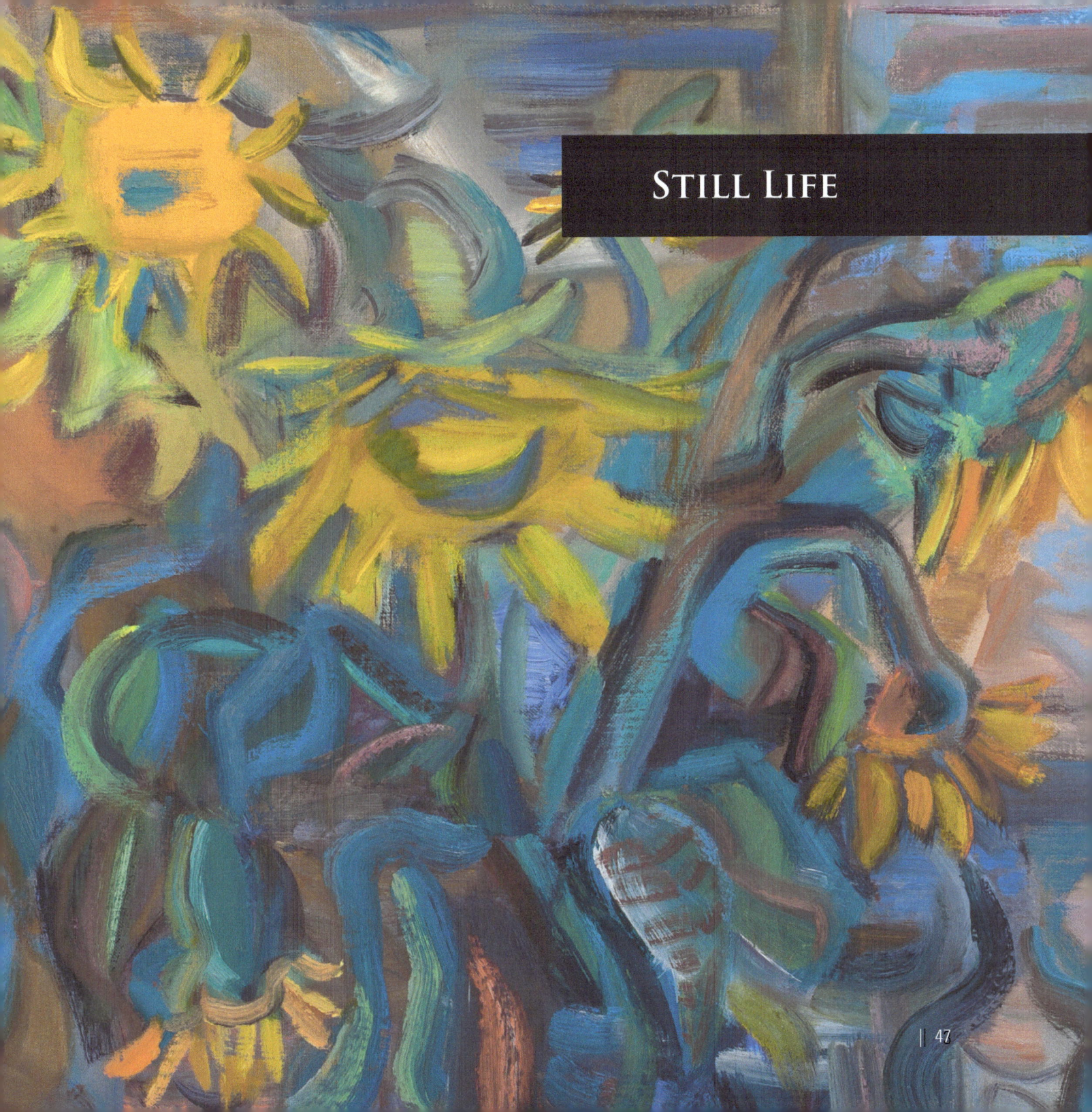

Geraniums and Cosmos

Oil on linen, 36 x 40 inches

2005

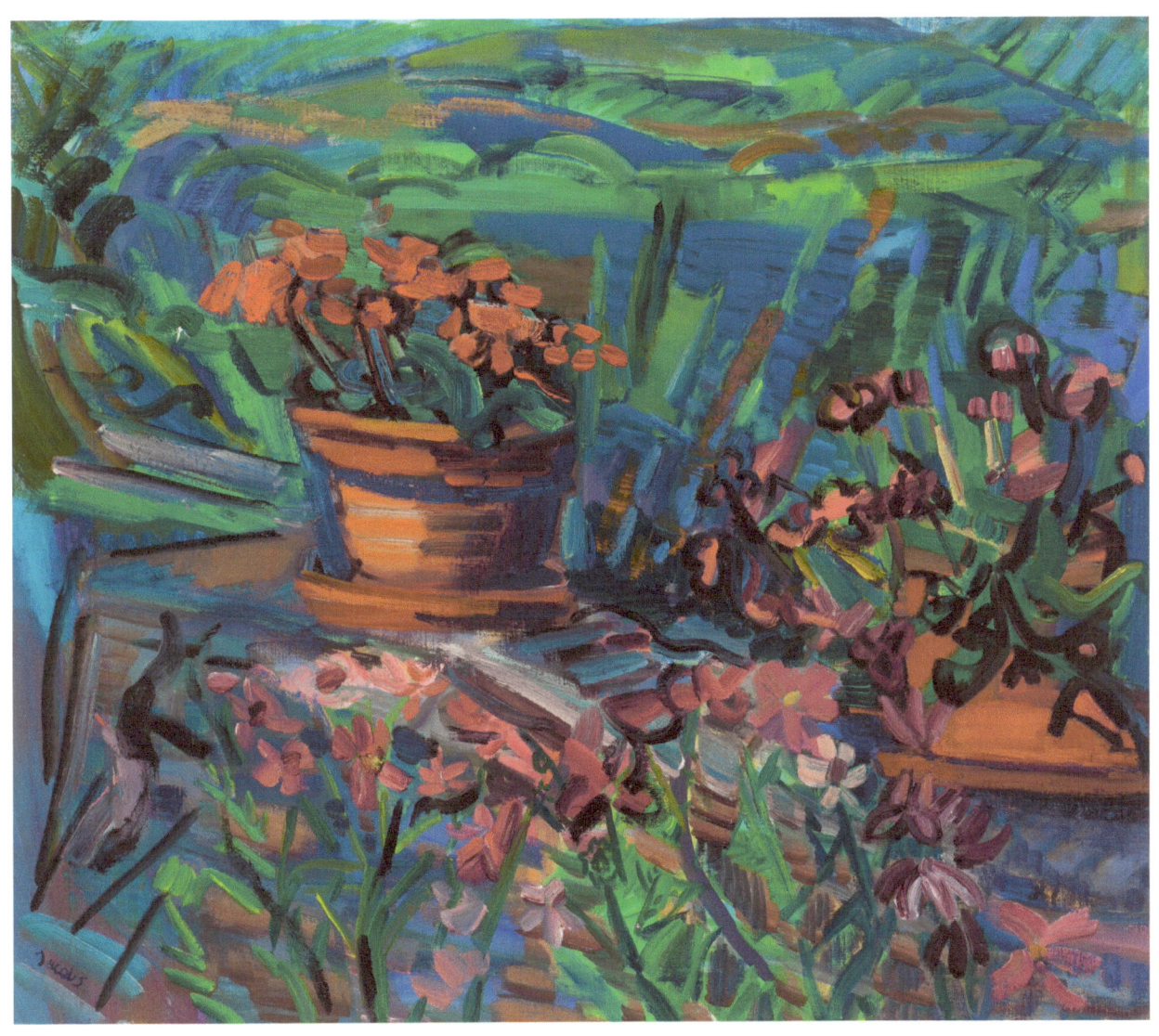

Sunflowers and Artichokes

Oil on linen, 30 x 34 inches

2005

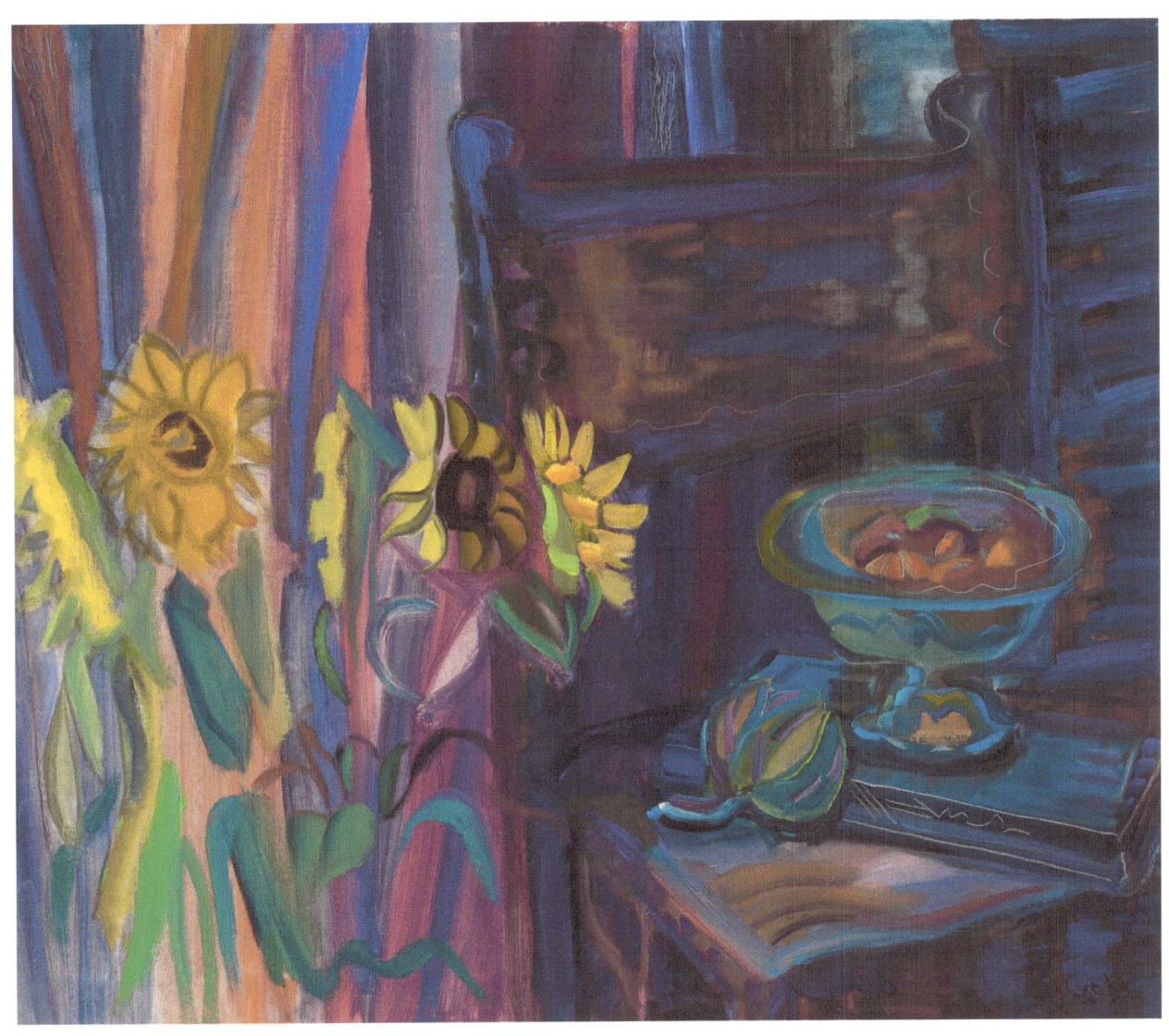

Sunflowers and Lemons

Oil on linen, 34 x 30 inches

2009

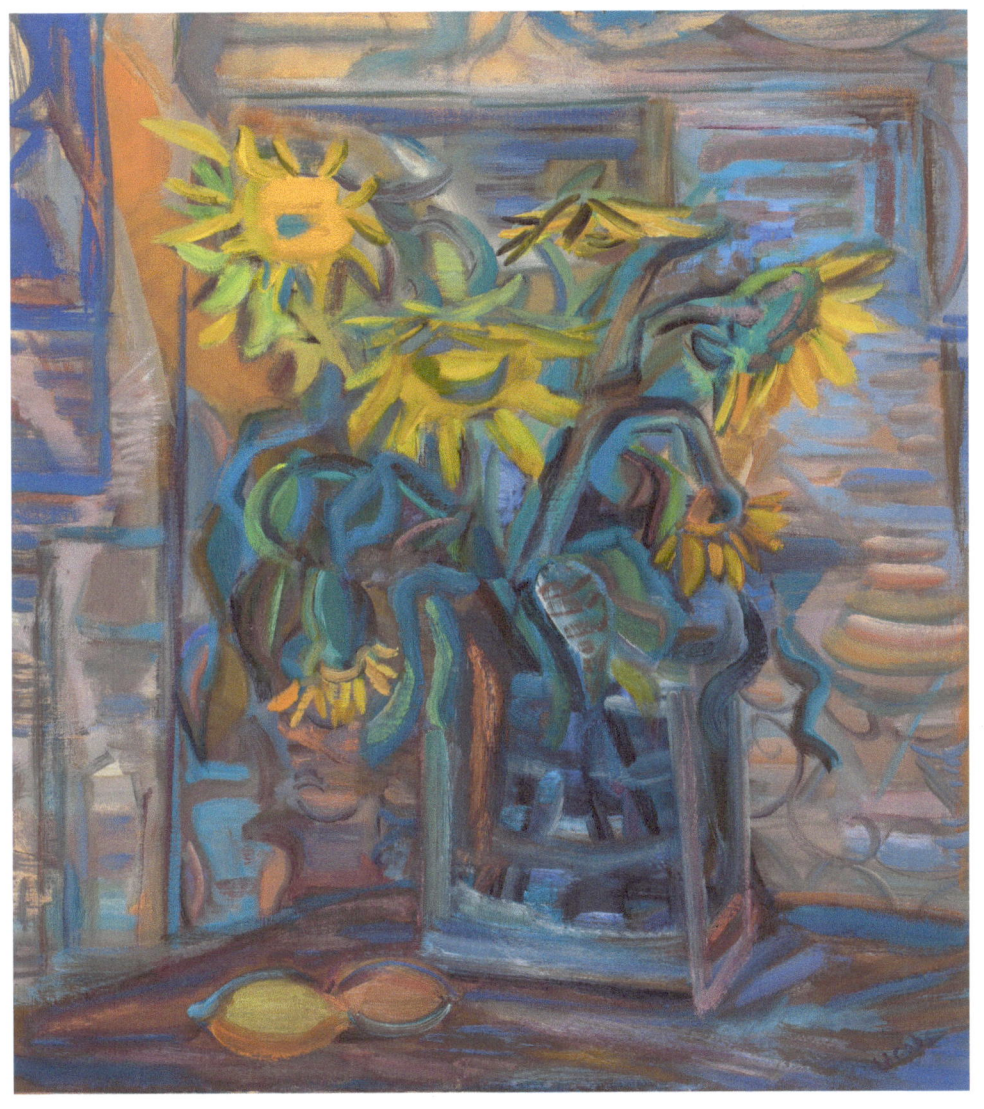

The Blue Pitcher

Oil on linen, 40 x 36 inches

2009

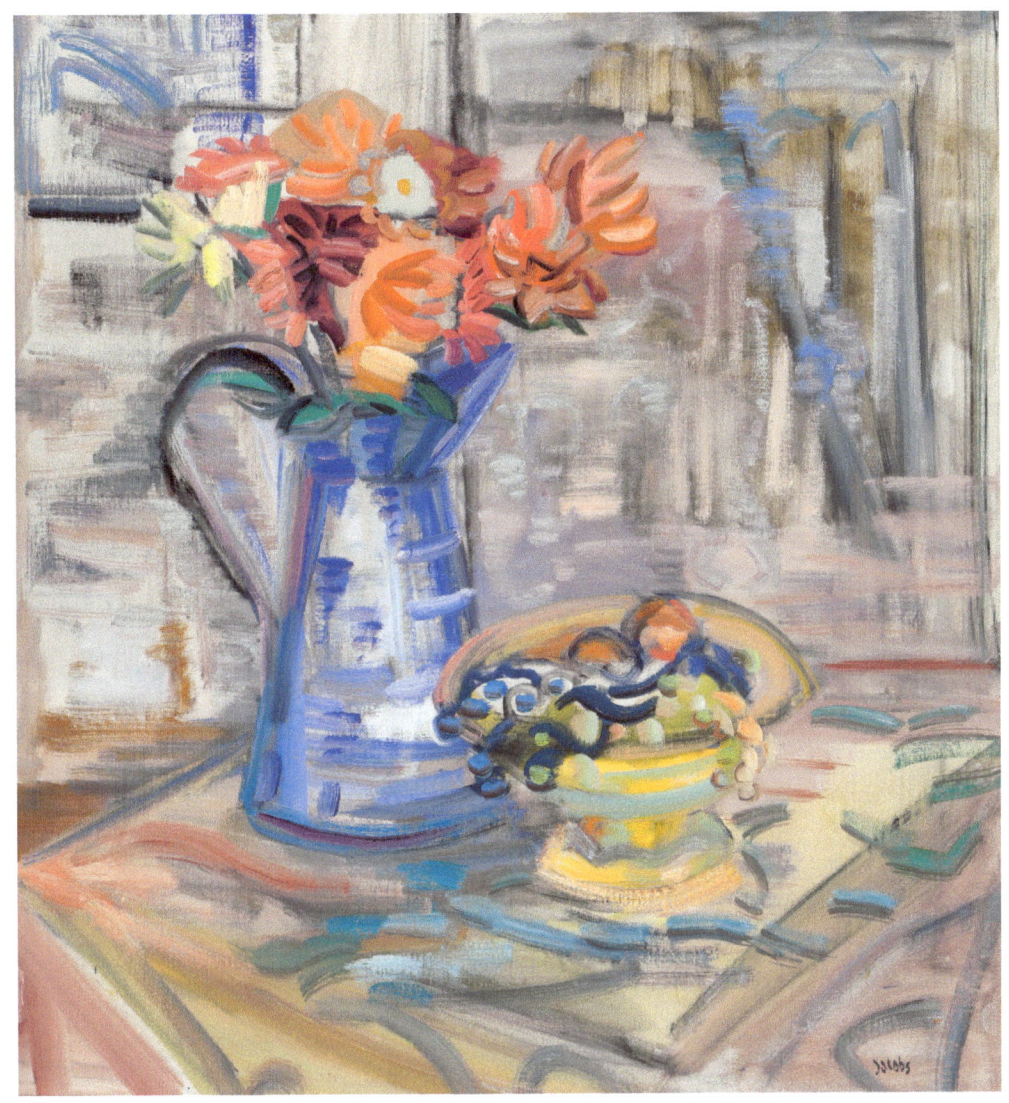

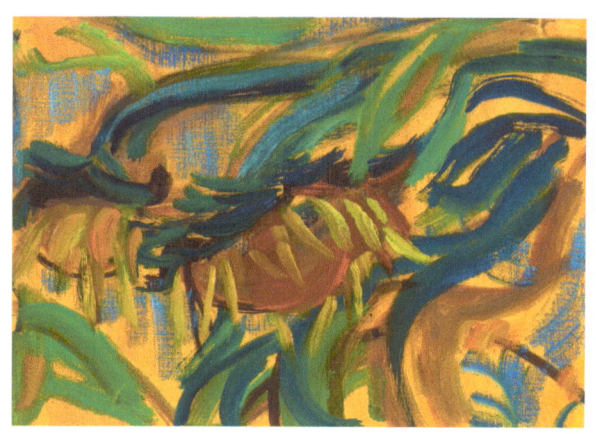

Sunflower 1

Oil on paper, 9 ½ x 13 inches

2010

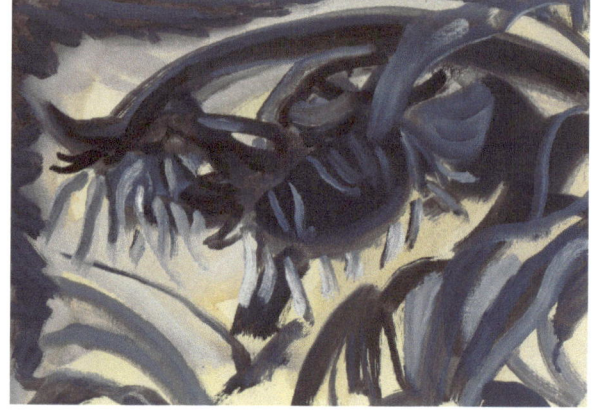

Sunflower 2

Oil on paper, 9 ½ x 13 inches

2010

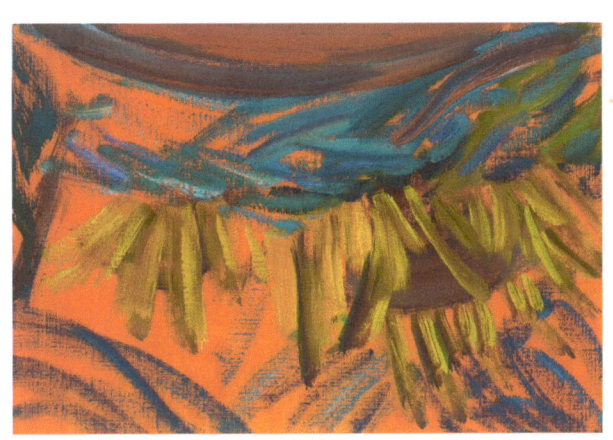

Sunflower 3

Oil on paper, 9 ½ x 13 inches

2010

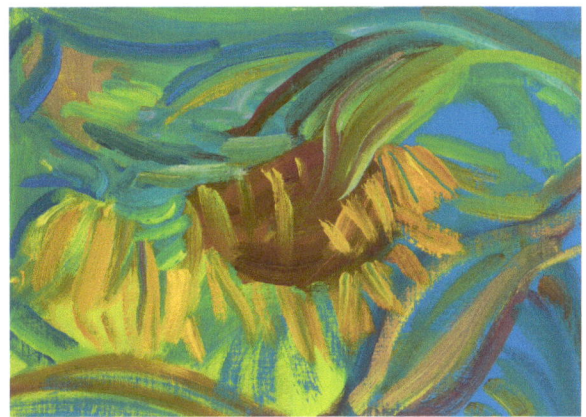

Sunflower 4

Oil on paper, 9 ½ x 13 inches

2010

Inside the Sunflower Field

Oil on linen, 30 x 34 inches

2010

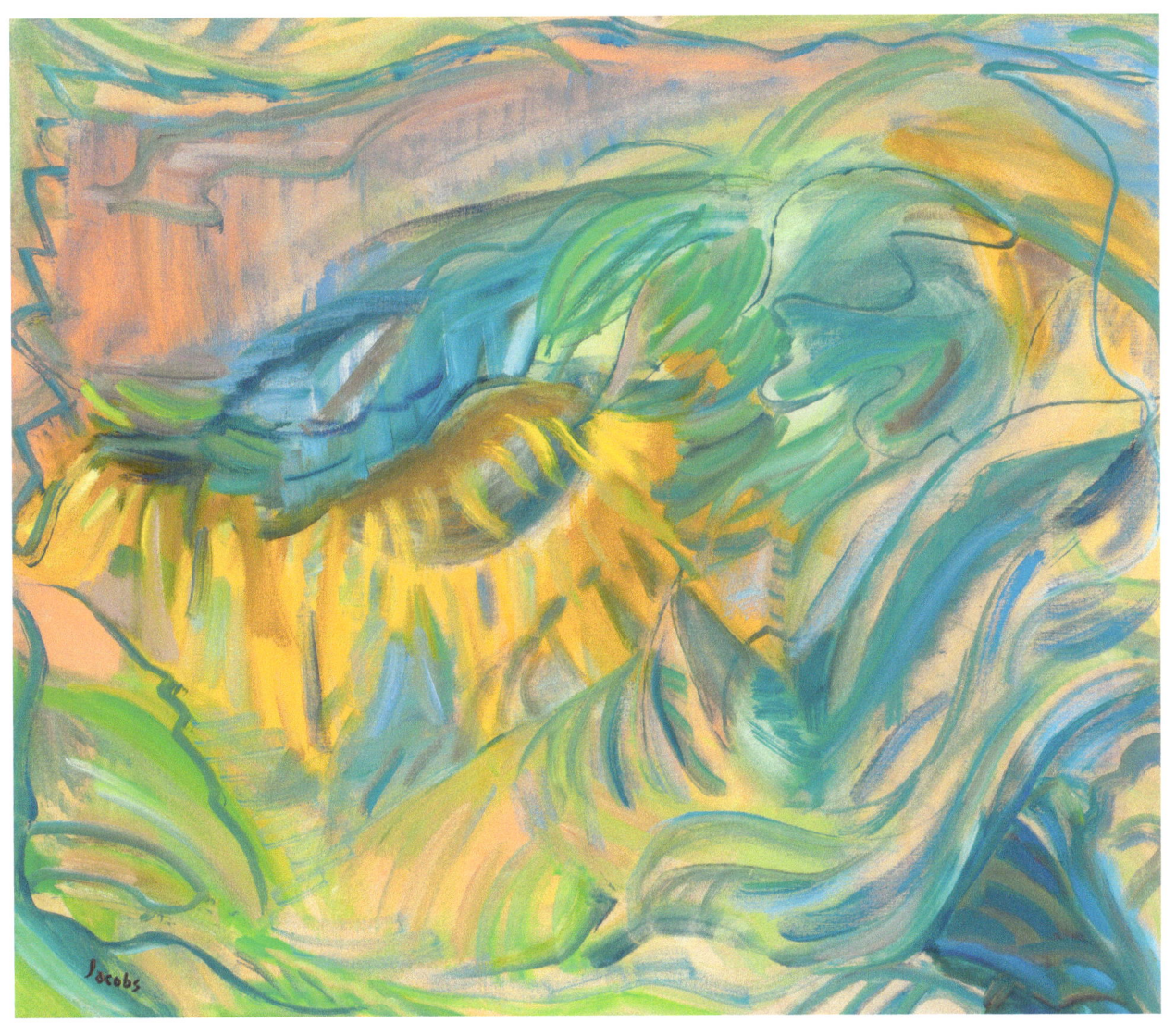

Still Life with Masks

Oil on linen, 54 x 44 inches

1999

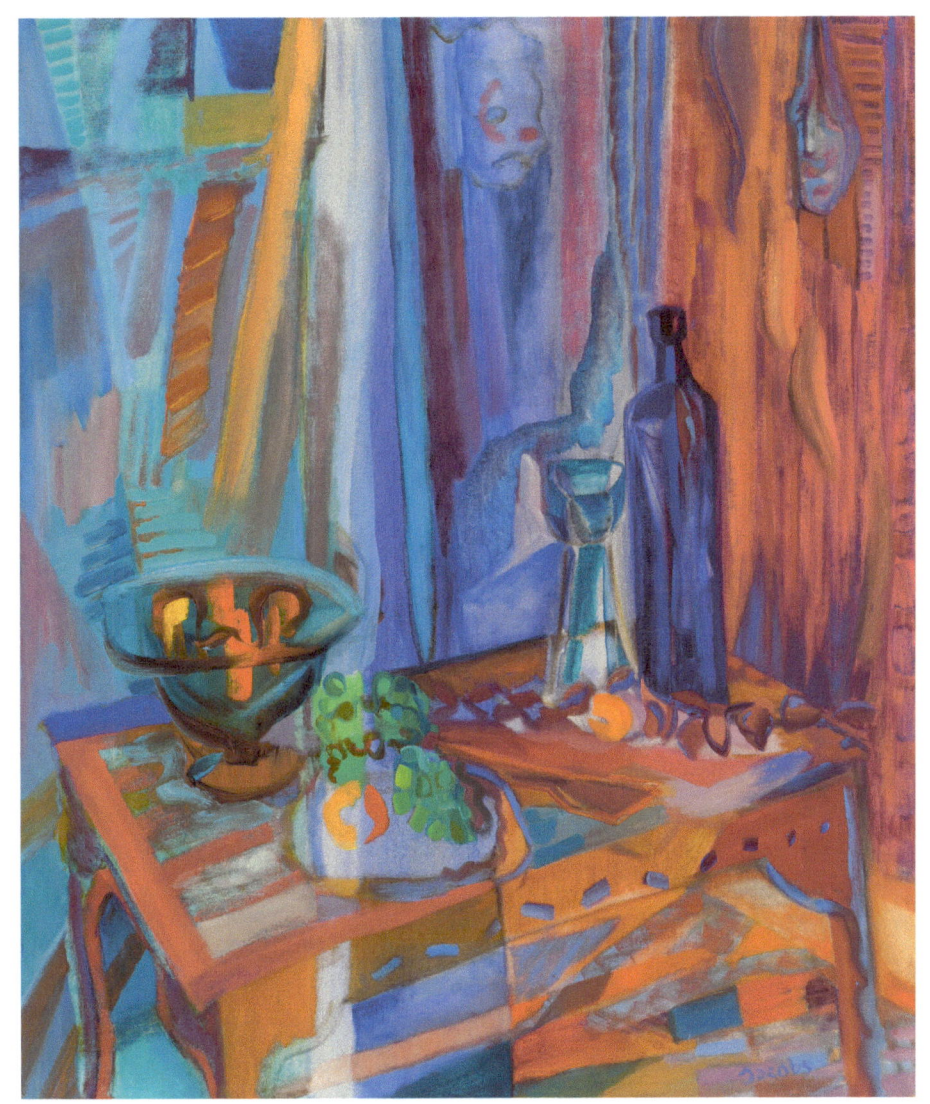

Turkish Bath, after Ingres (detail)

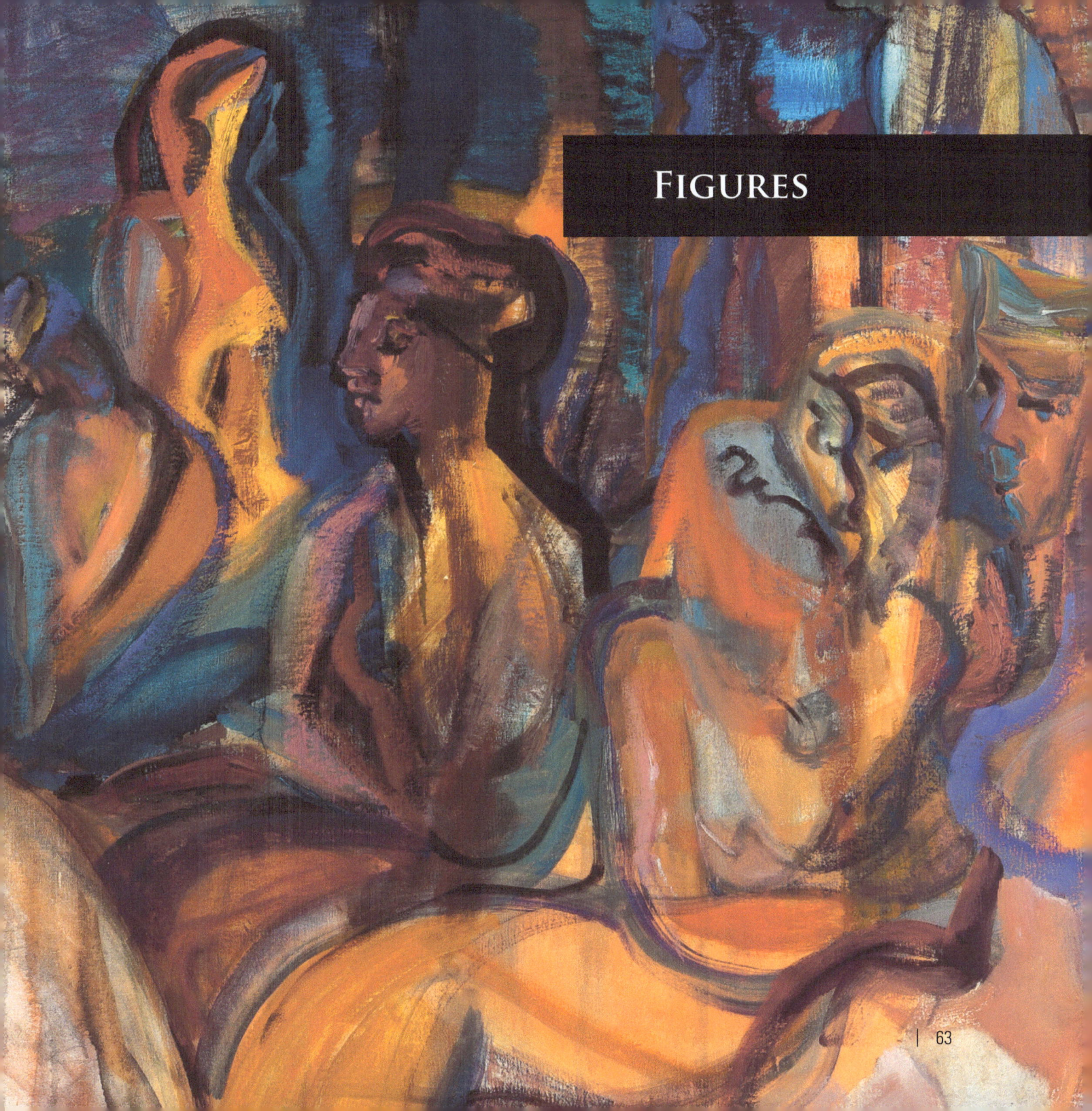

FIGURES

Figure at Paris Window

Oil on linen, 36 x 30 inches

2008

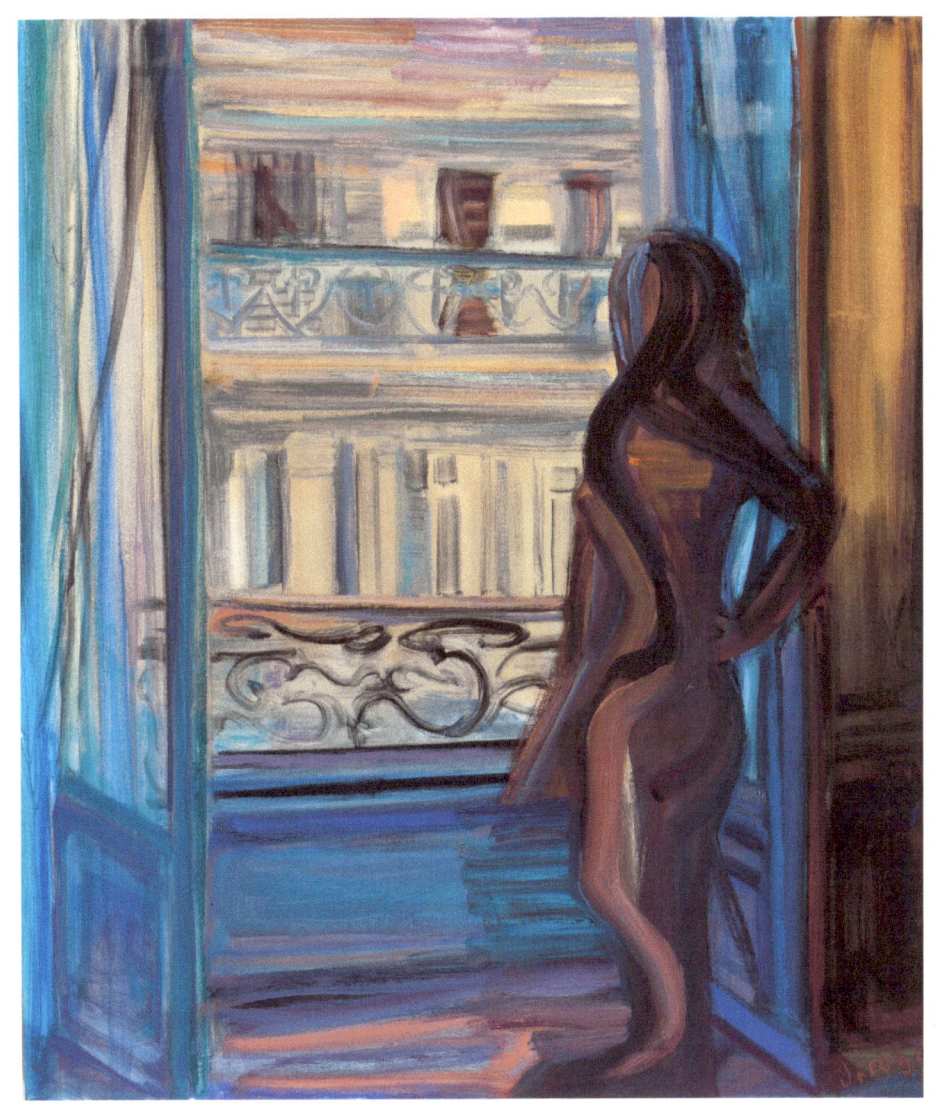

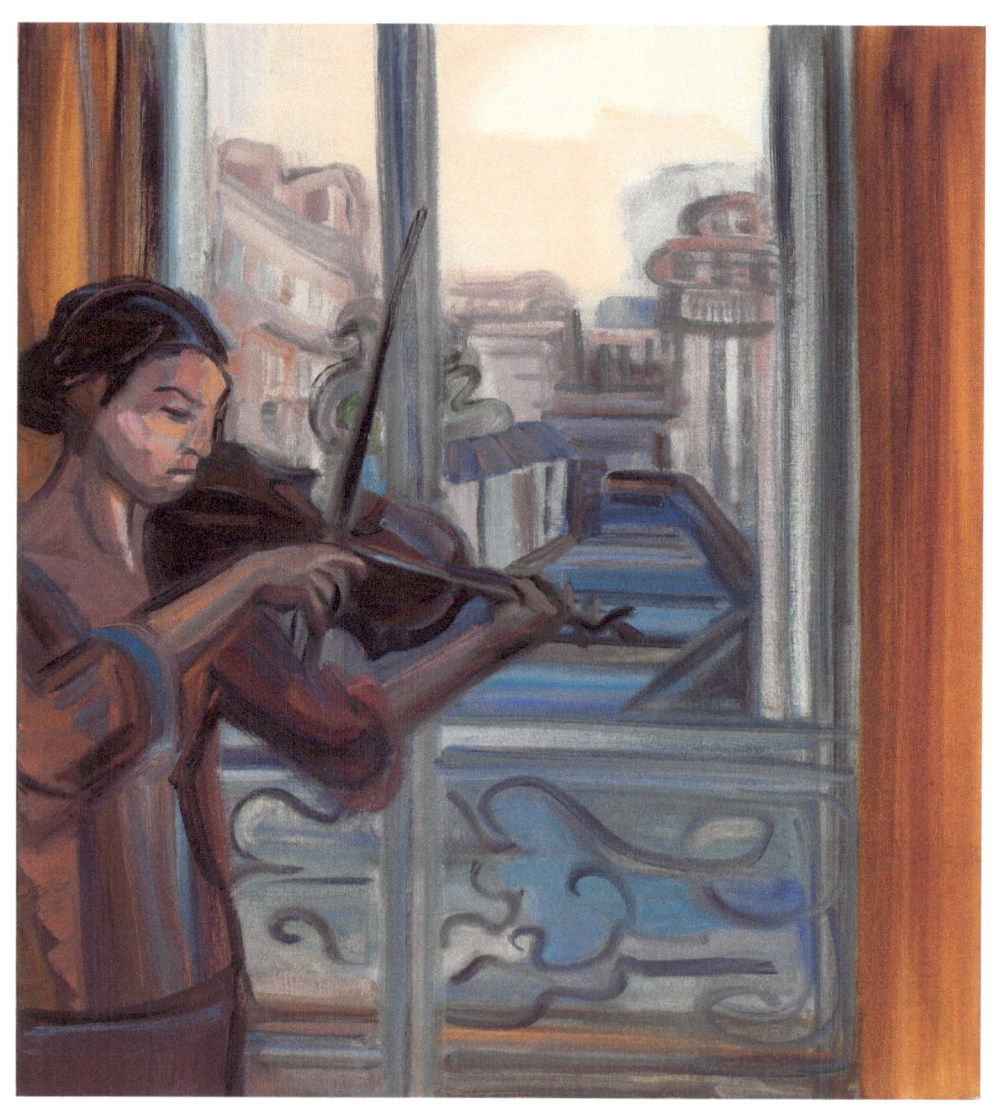

Maya in Paris

Oil on linen, 34 x 30 inches

2008

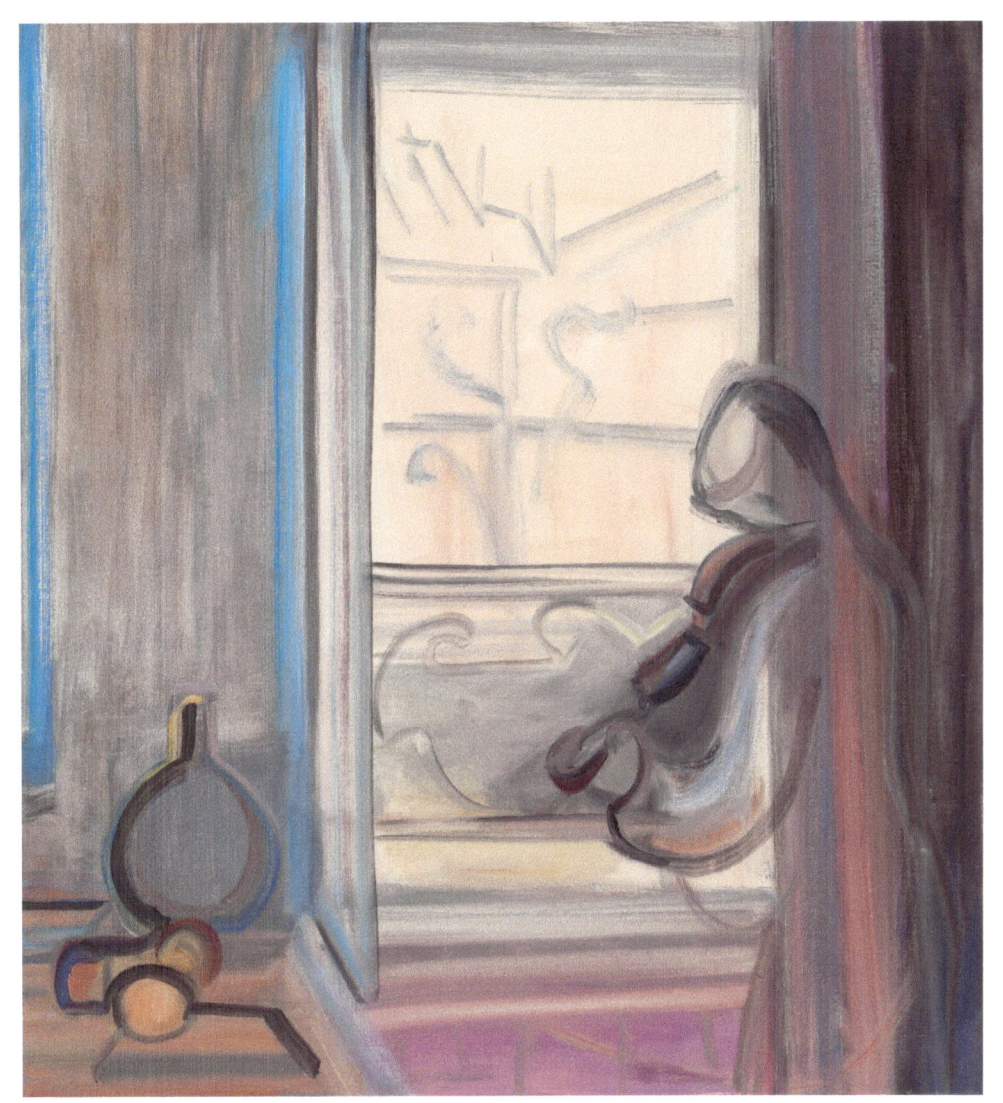

Paris Musician

Oil on linen, 34 x 30 inches

2008

Paris Window

Oil on linen, 34 x 30 inches

2008

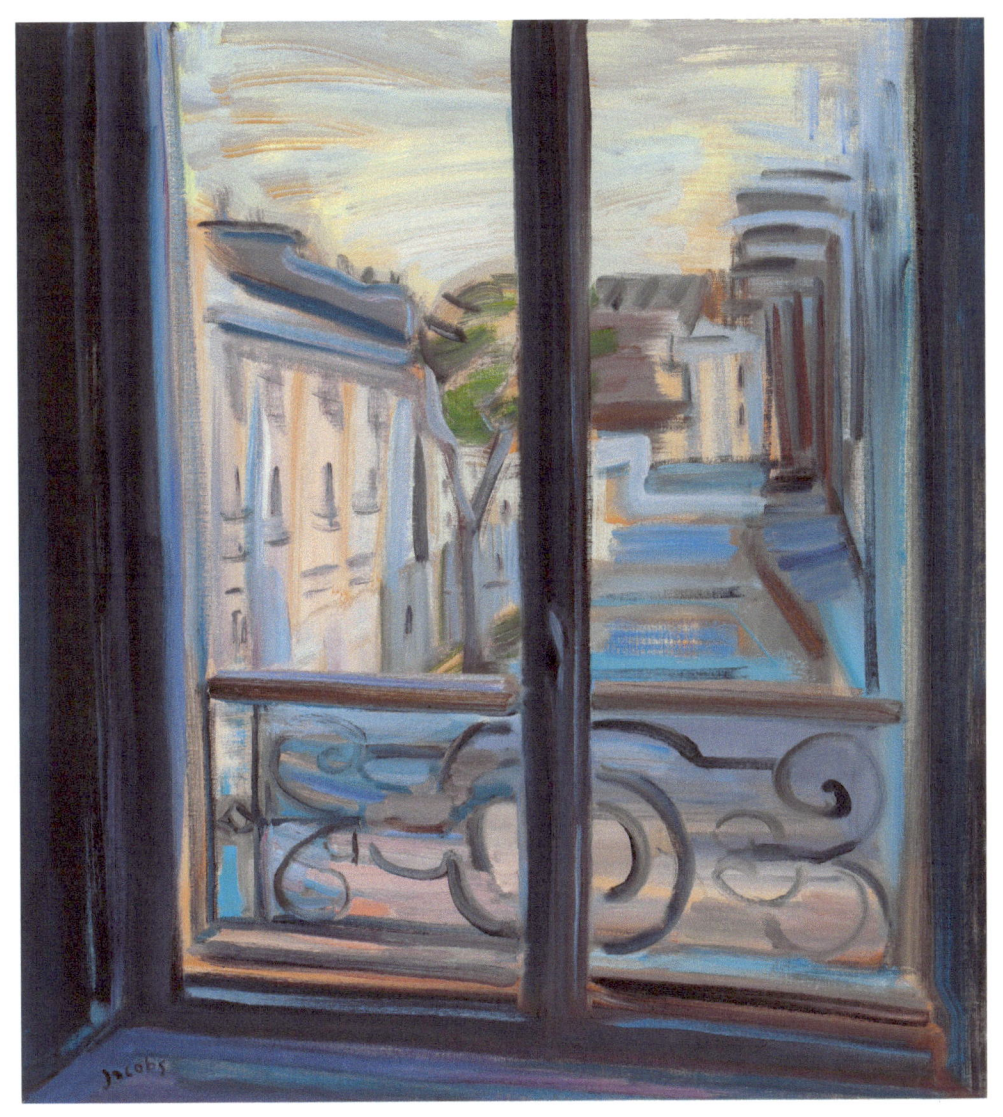

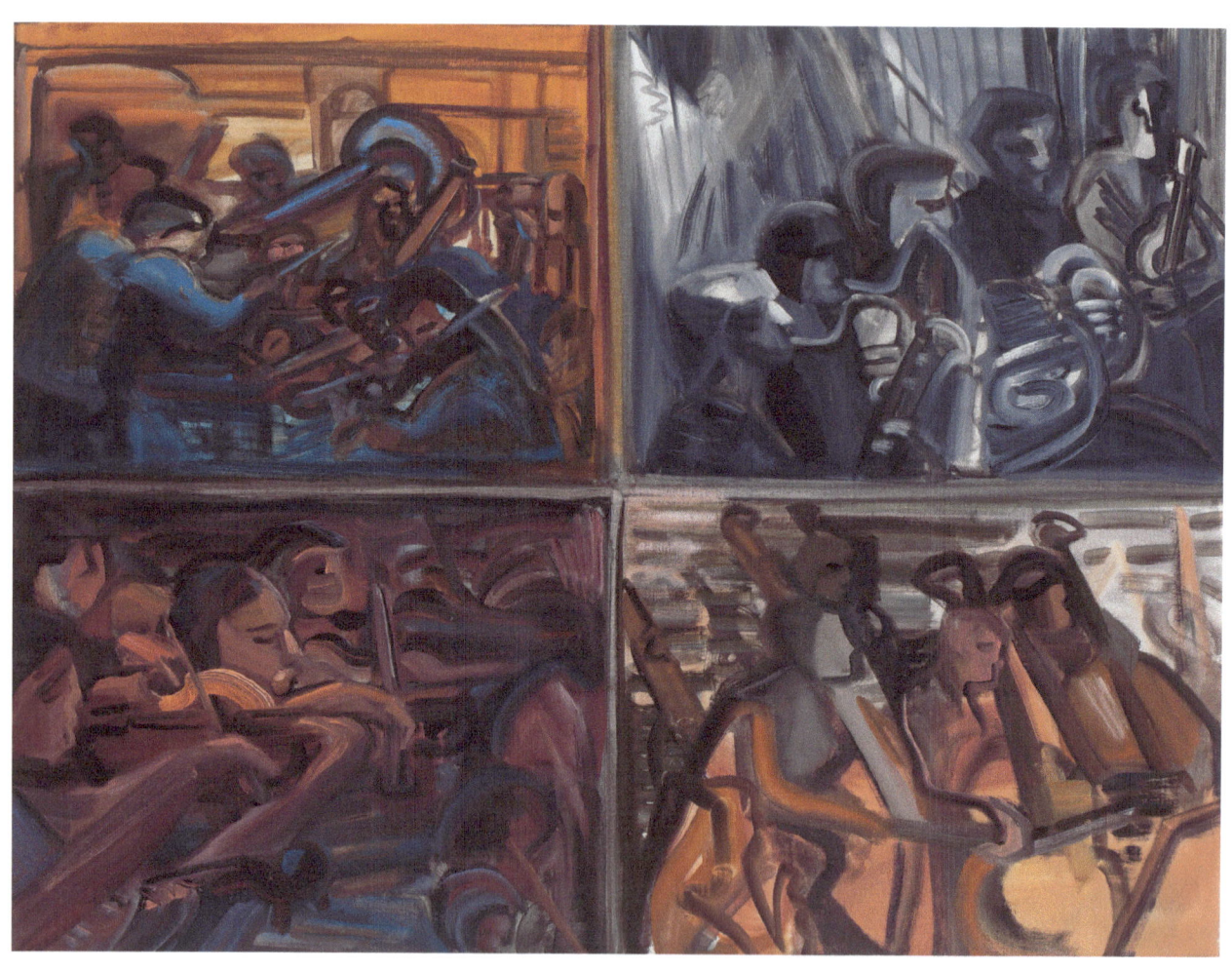

Musicians Quartet 1

Oil on linen, 28 x 36 inches

2008

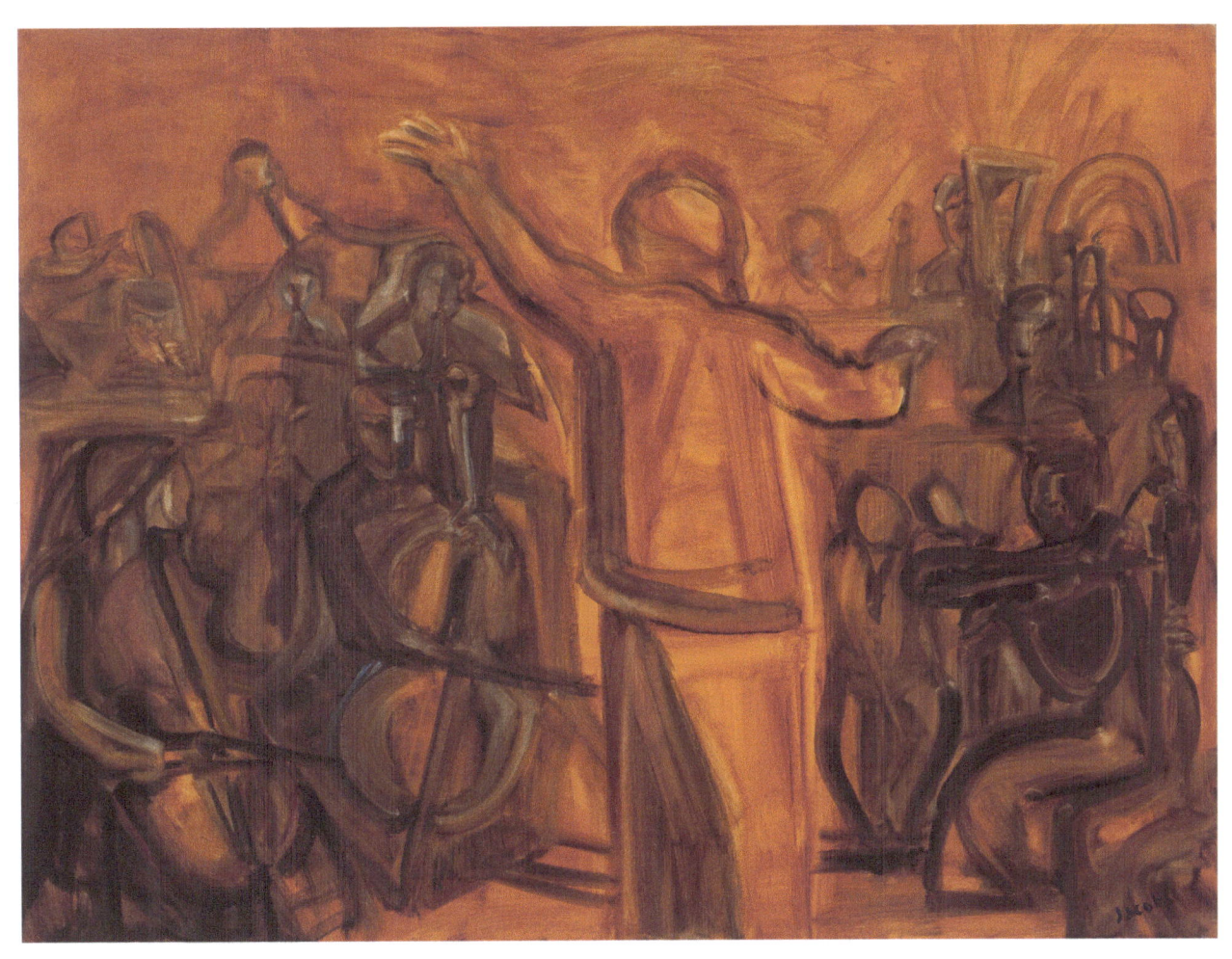

Maestro Barenboim

Oil on linen, 28 x 36 inches

2008

Musicians Quartet 2

Oil on linen, 28 x 36 inches

2008

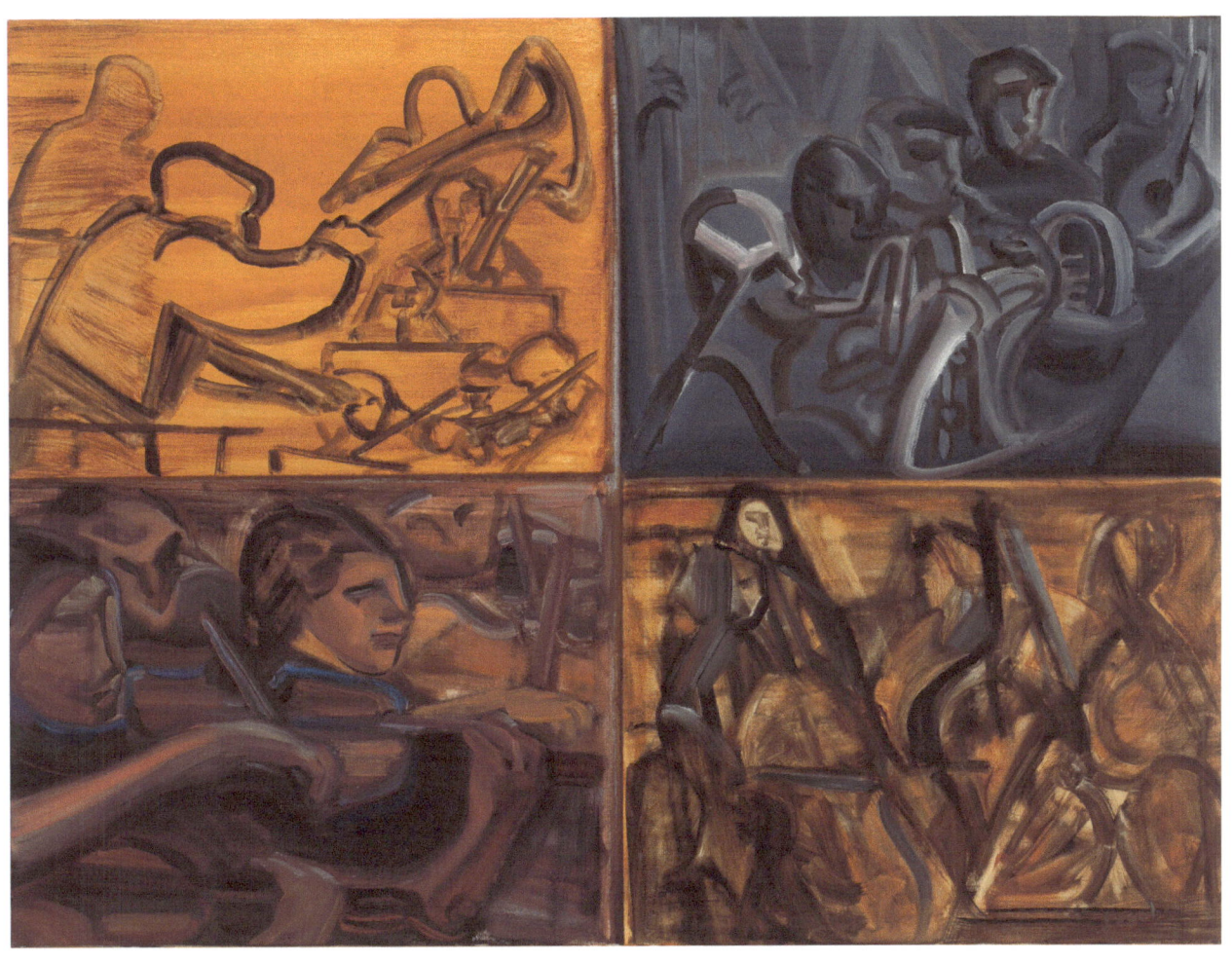

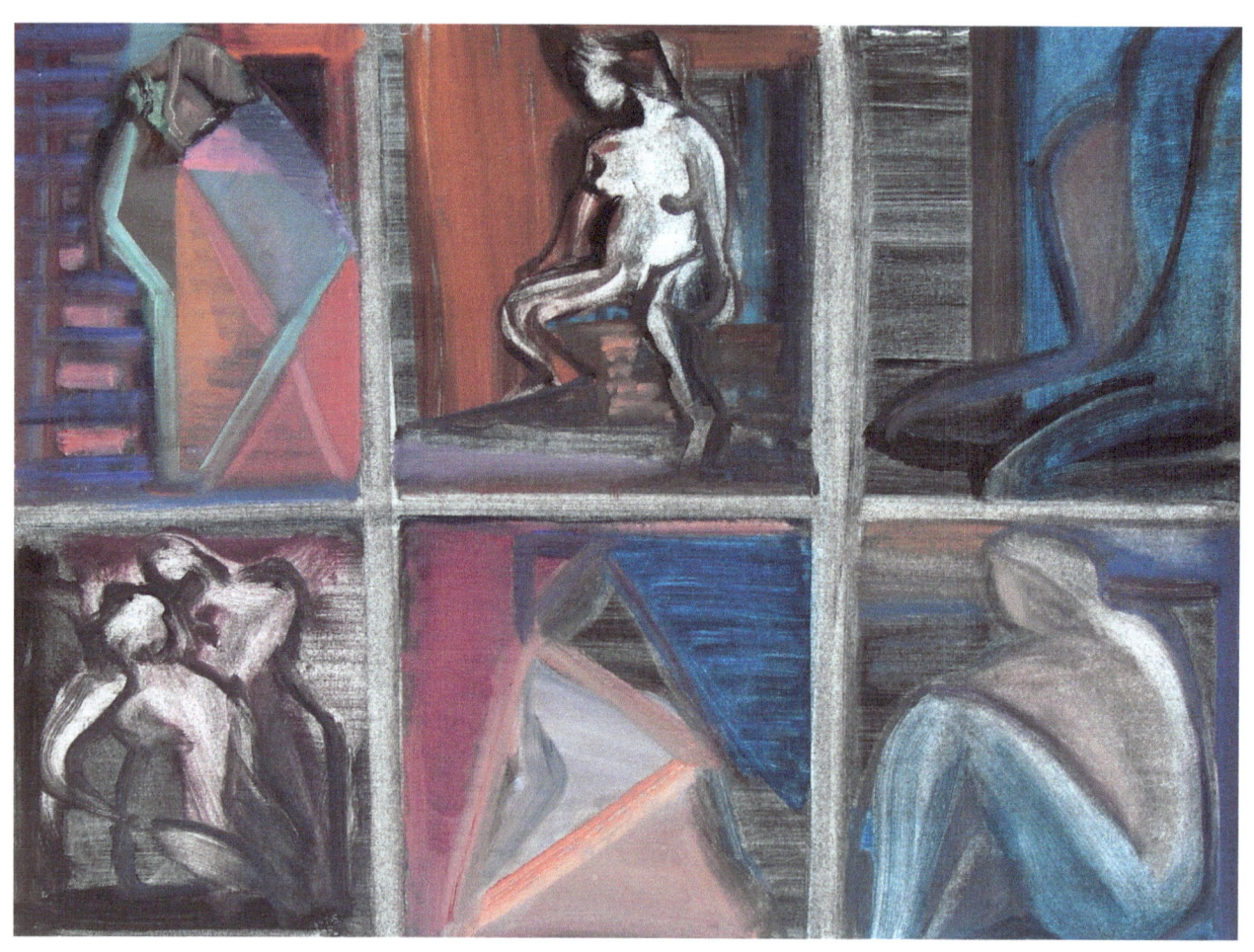

Figures series 2

Oil on paper, 19 5/8 x 25 1/2 inches

2008

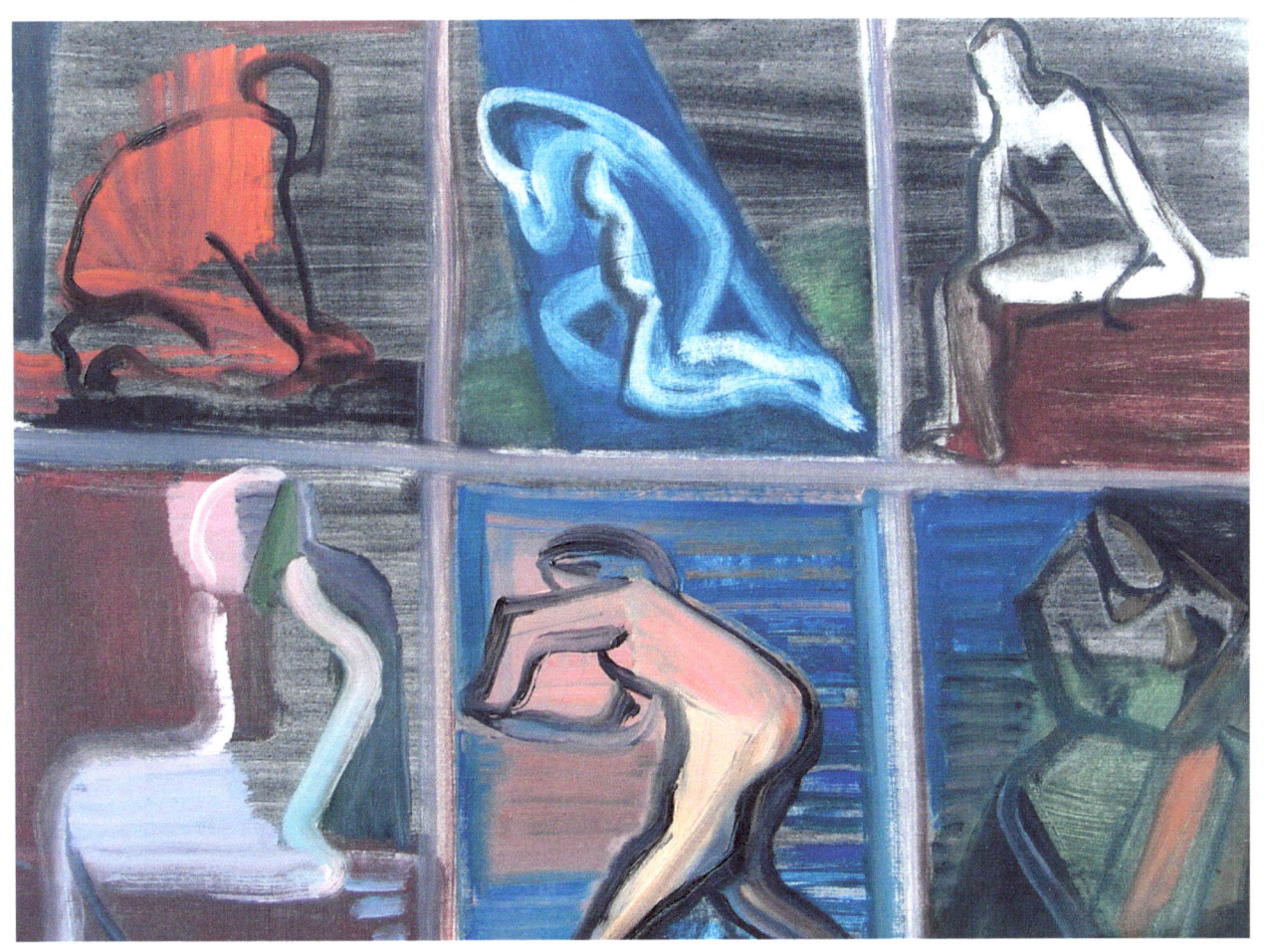

Figures series 1

Oil on paper, 19 5/8 x 25 1/2 inches

2008

Turkish Bath

Oil on canvas, 25 x 30 inches

1999

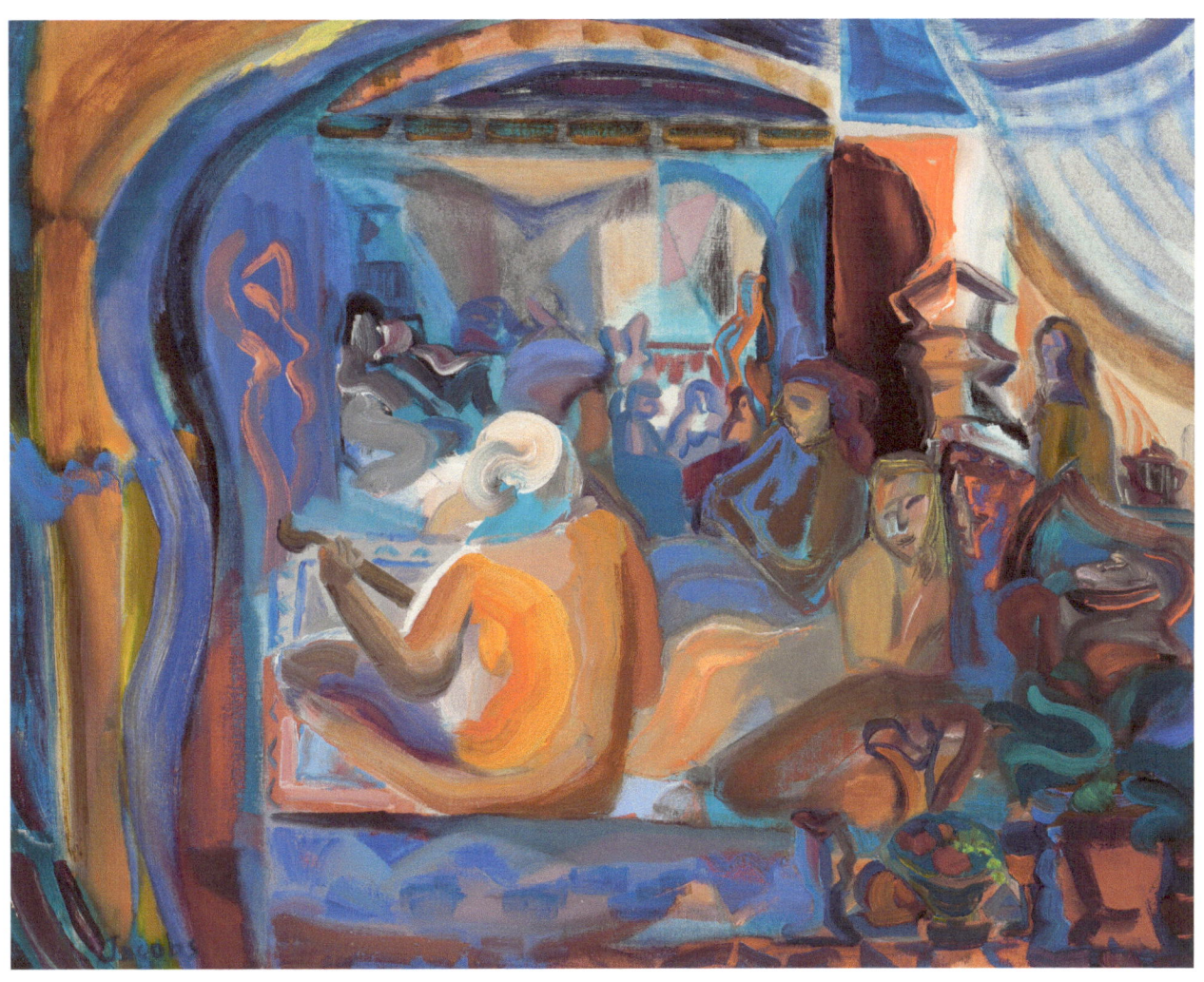

Turkish Bath Quartet

Oil on canvas, 30 x 30 inches

2008

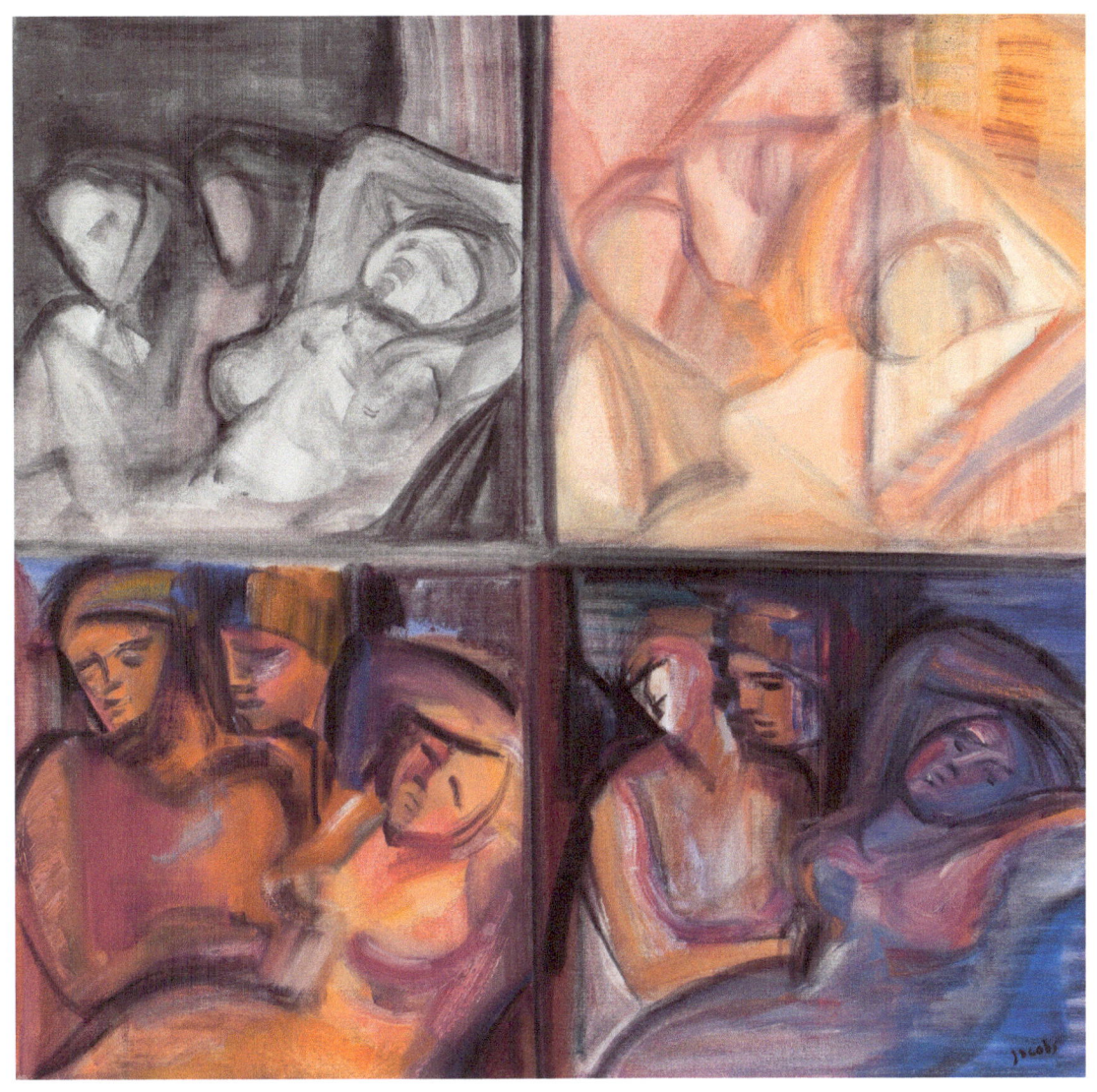

Turkish Bath, after Ingres

Oil on canvas, 60 x 72 inches

1999

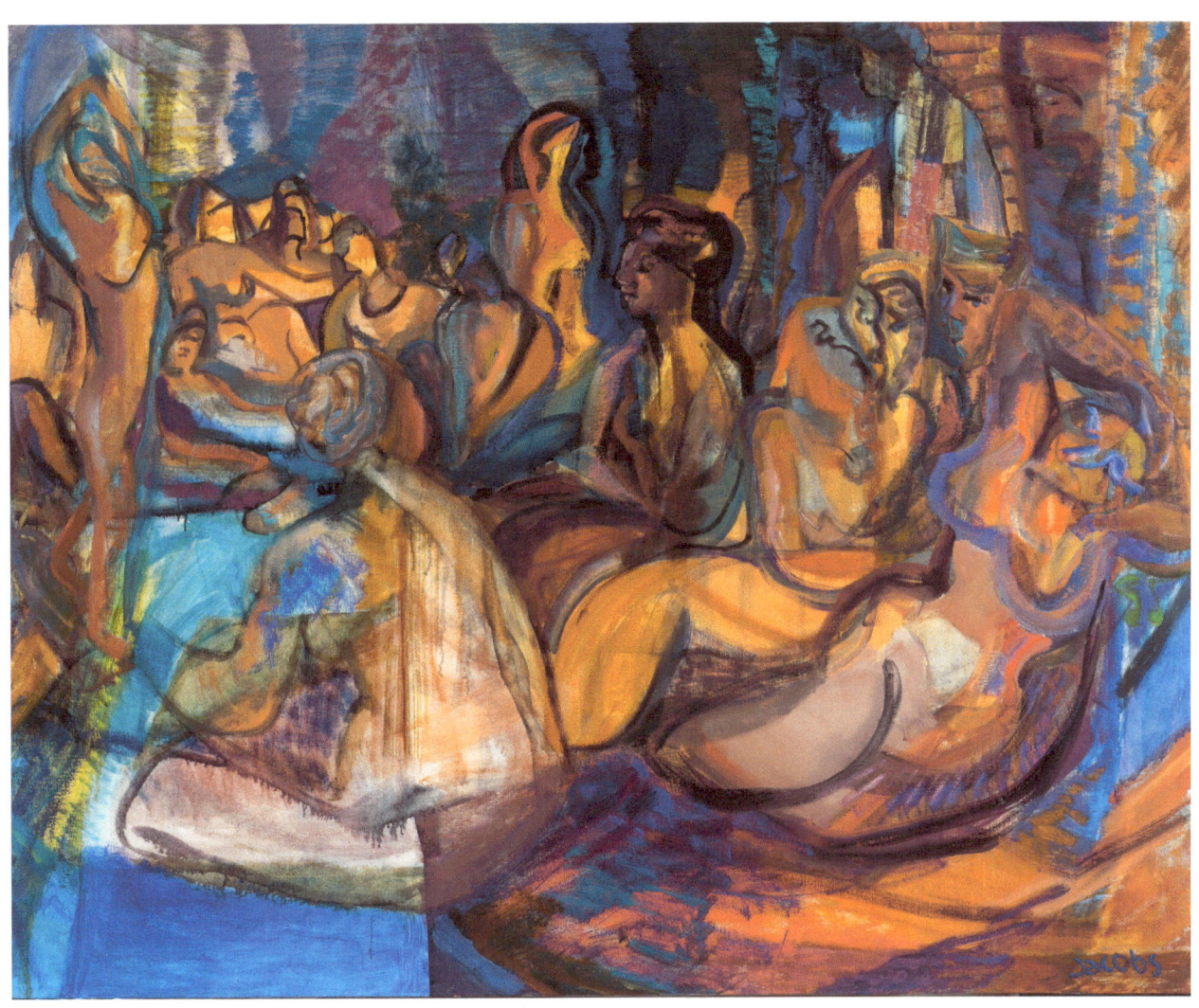

Gourdon Honey Vendor

Oil on linen, 30 x 34 inches

2005

82 |

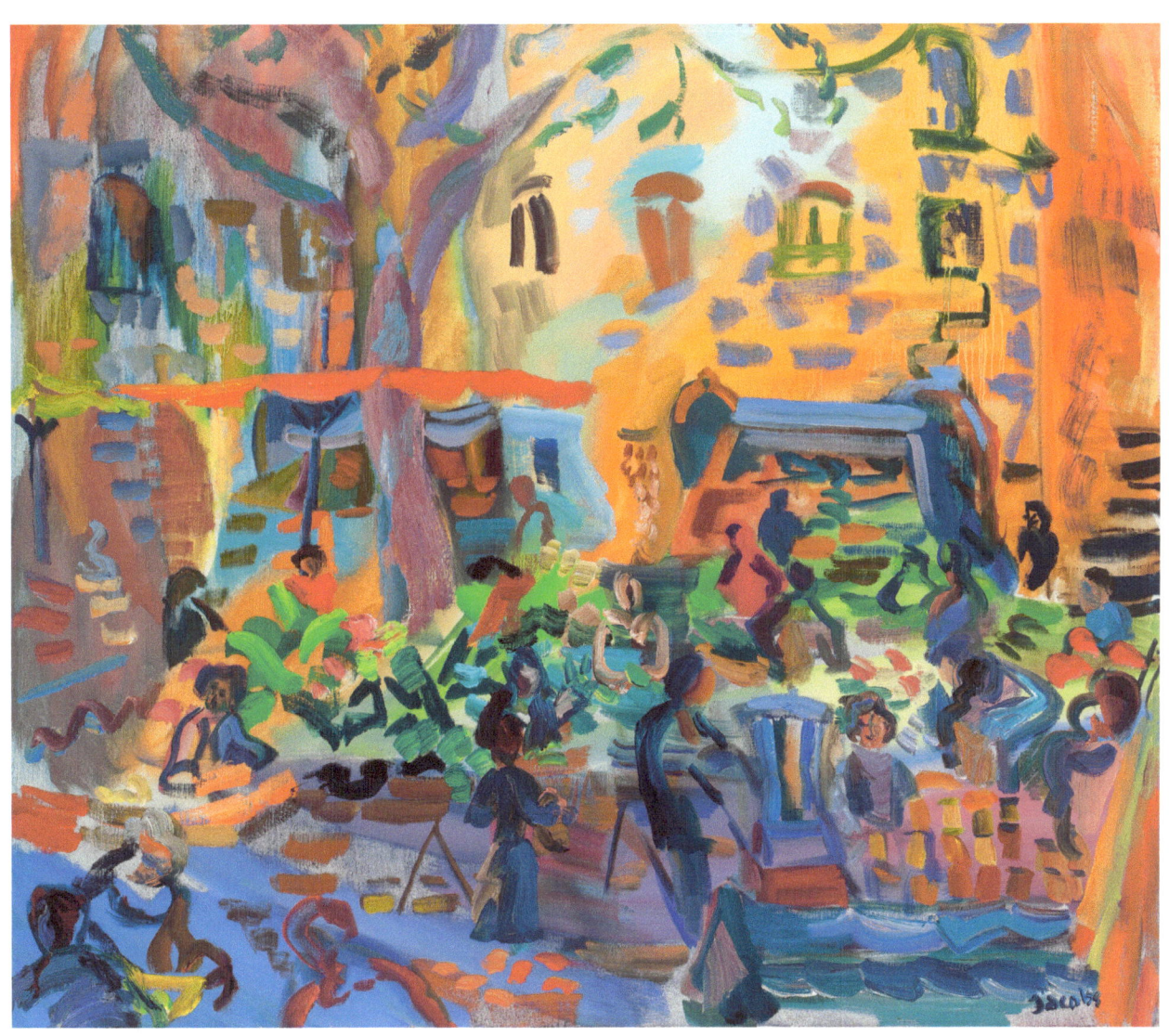

At the Market

Oil on linen, 30 x 34 inches

2007

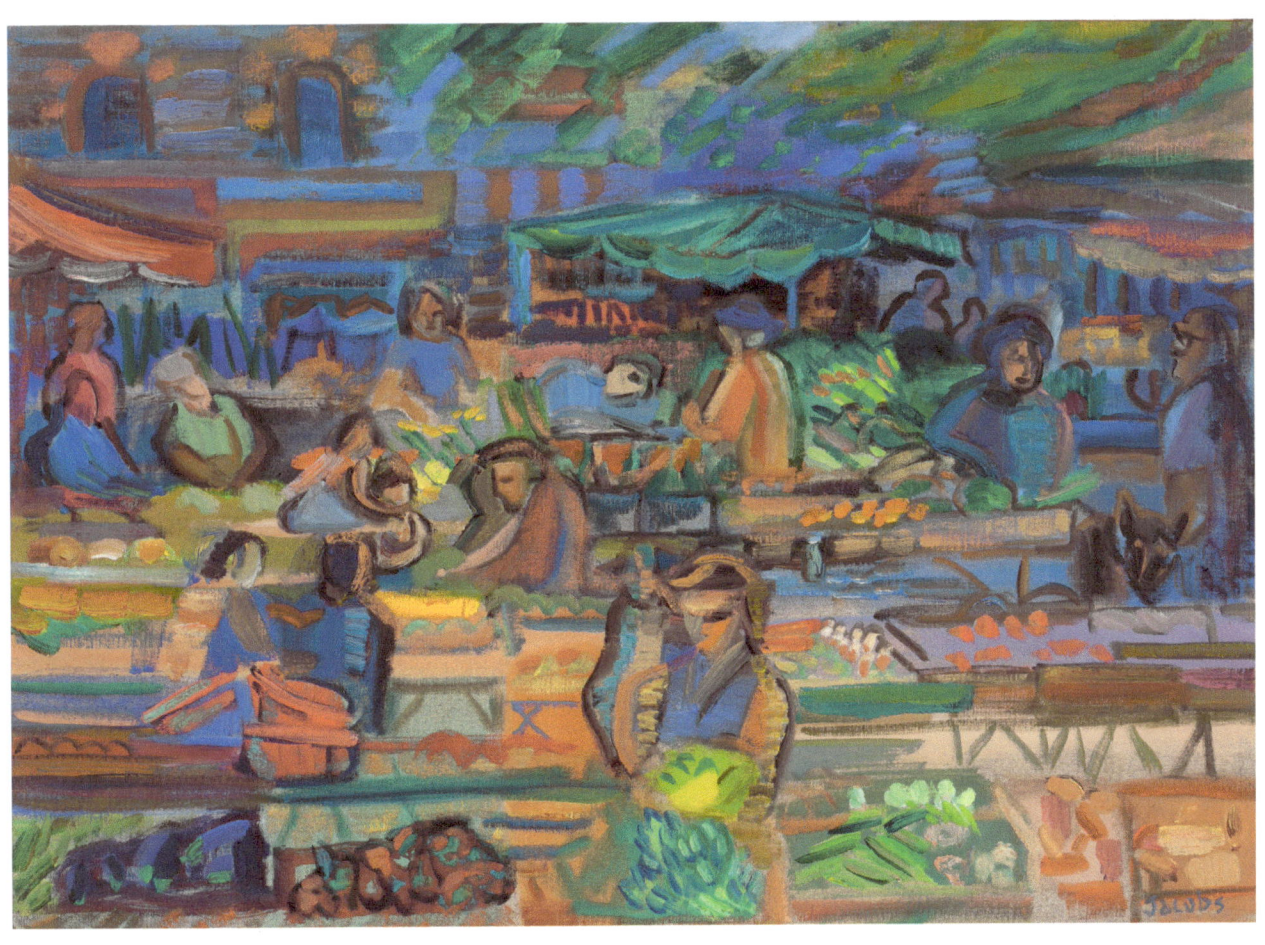

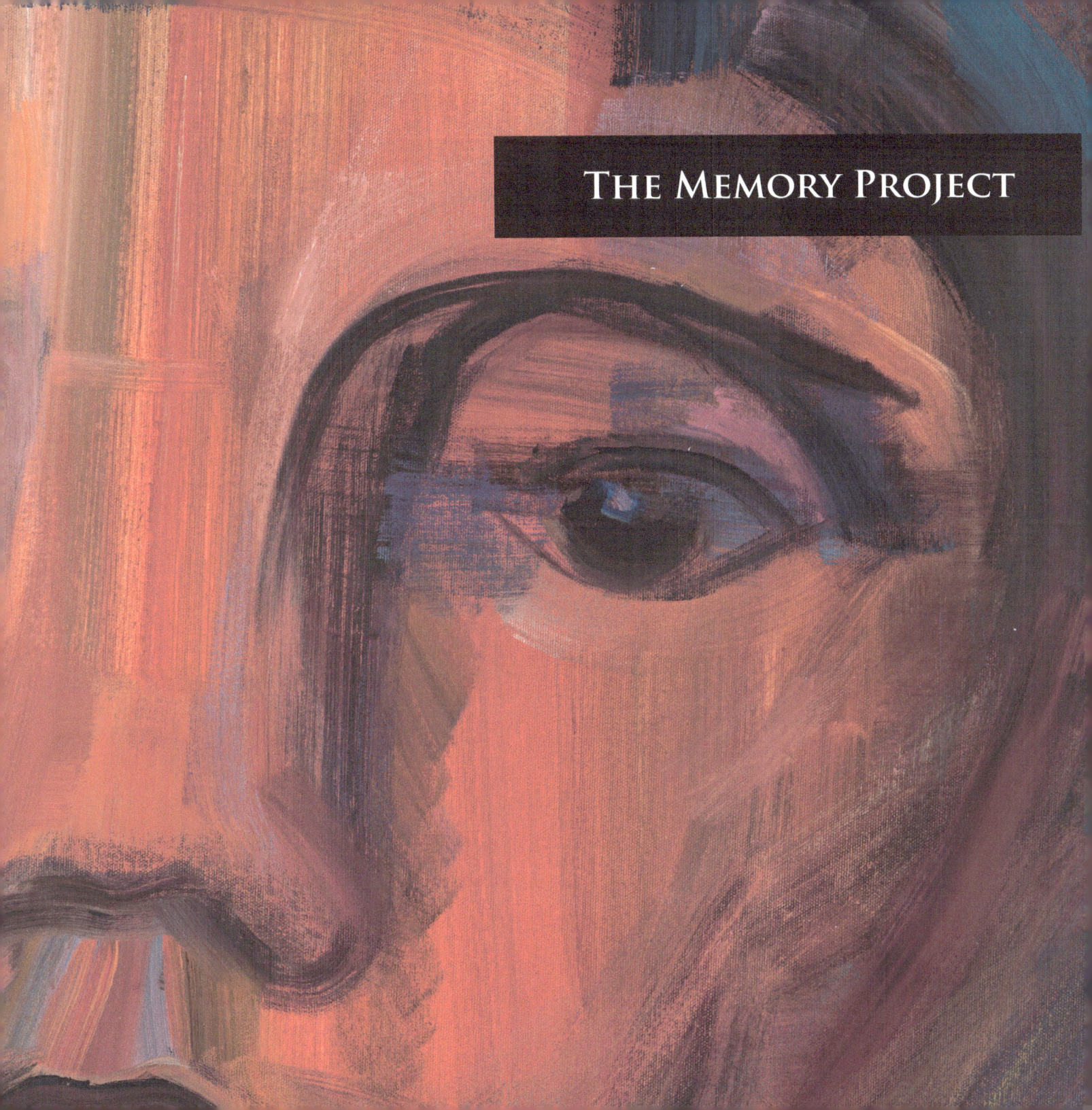

THE MEMORY PROJECT

THE MEMORY PROJECT

A boy named Kalman Huberman vanished during the Holocaust. Like more than one and half million other Jewish children, his life was cut brutally short. This particular boy was my mother's beloved younger brother, my uncle. She told me stories about him when I was a child and I used to dream that I would find him—to restore for my mother a piece of her lost past. Several years ago, I conceived of an art exhibit built around Kalman.

I painted his portrait over and over again, videotaping each one. The Memory Project installation uses nine video monitors—one for each painting. It reveals the process of how the paintings evolved—falling apart and coming together until the form of the head was realized. The counterpoint to the painting process is my mother telling Kalman's story, just as I heard it throughout my childhood.

Together with Laurie Weisman, co-creator of the exhibition, I'm developing classroom materials so that teachers and students can use creativity to connect to history—from the specific history of the Holocaust to their own family stories.

The Memory Project is about recapturing something that was destroyed. Loss happens to all of us. How do we cope with it? How do we connect to the past and to each other? How do we transform trauma? This art installation's construction and content is meant to illustrate the transformative power of art and remembrance.

The Memory Project is touring museums and Holocaust centers around the world.

WWW.MEMORYPROJECTPRODUCTIONS.COM

Memory Project Installation, multi-media, 2007
Nathan D. Rosen Museum, Boca Raton, Florida

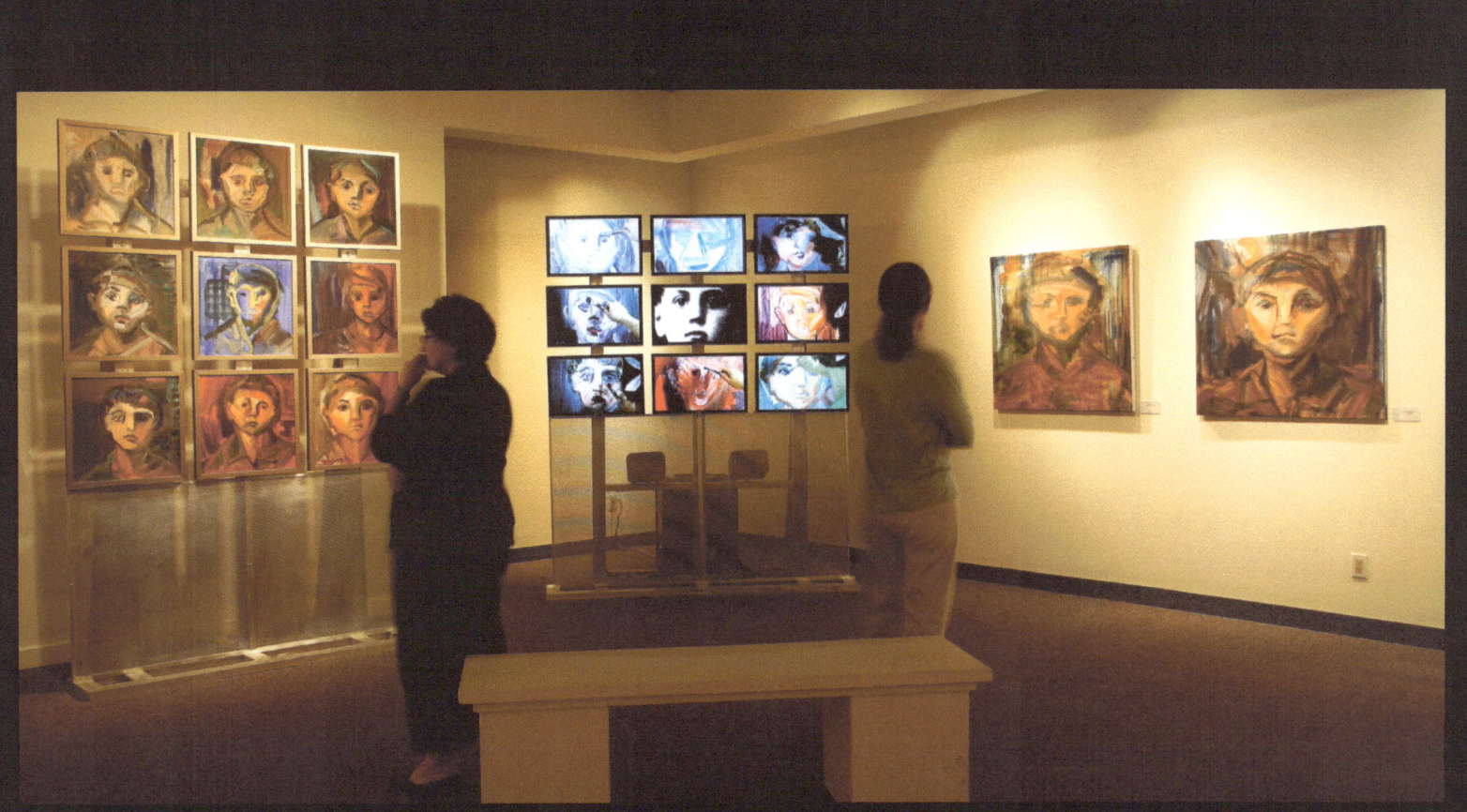

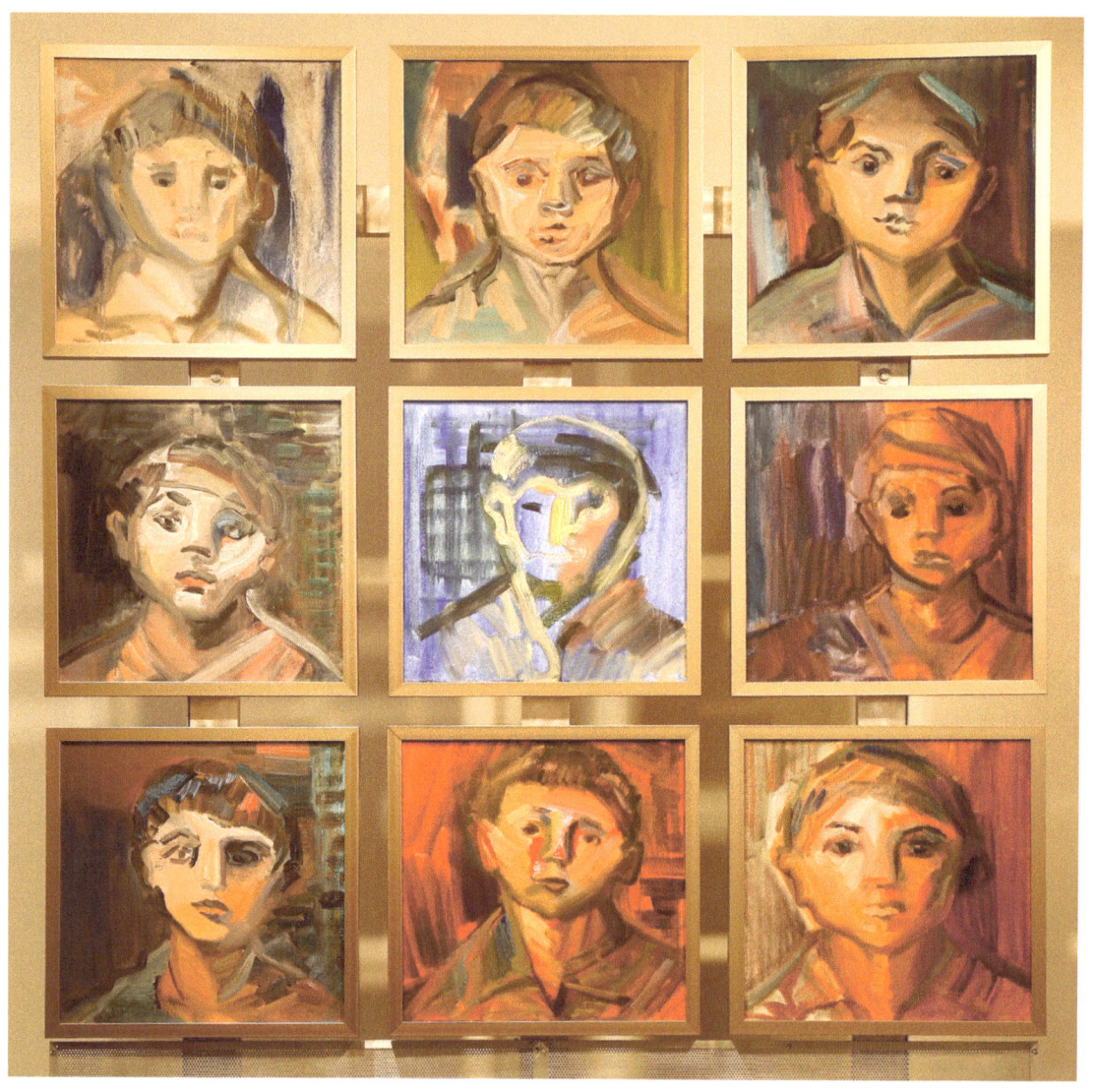

Kalman 1-9

Oil on linen, 18 x 18 inches, 2006. Nine portraits of my uncle Kalman, who disappeared during the Holocaust.

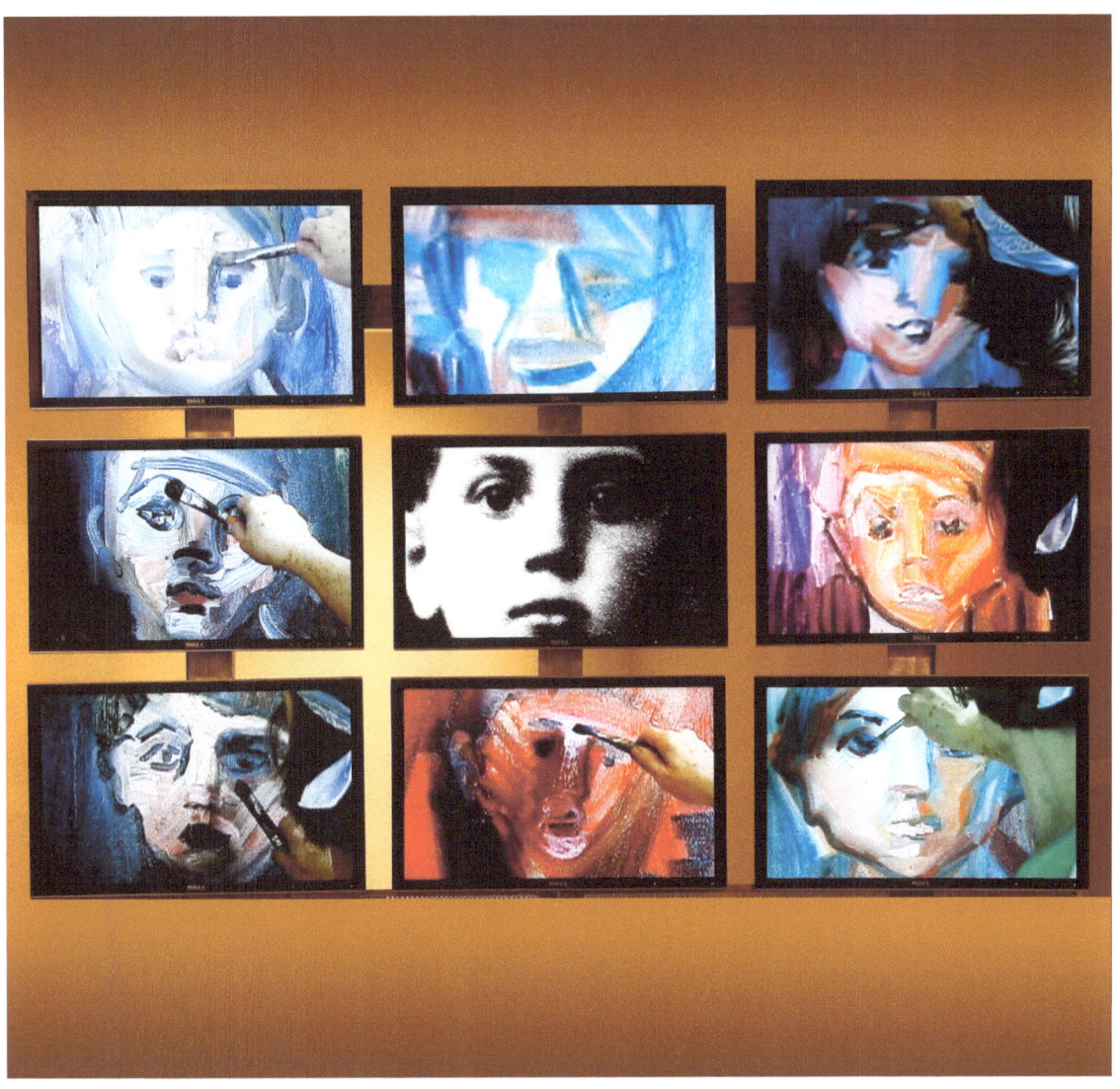

Video Installation

Nine video monitors play a thirteen-minute video loop showing the Kalman portraits being made.

The process is interwoven with my mother recounting her brother Kalman's story.

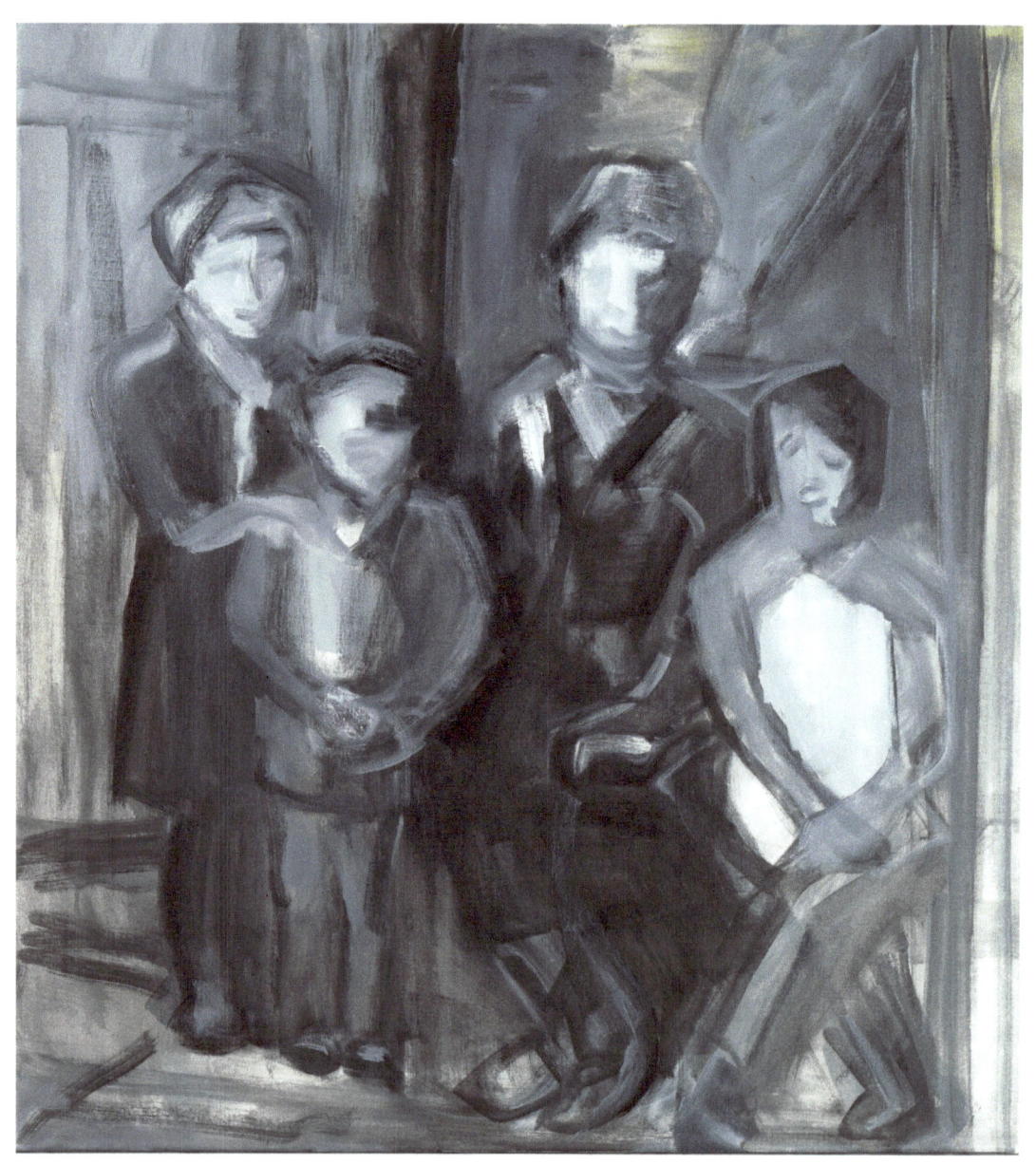

Huberman Family Portrait Black and White

Oil on linen, 34 x 30 inches, 2010

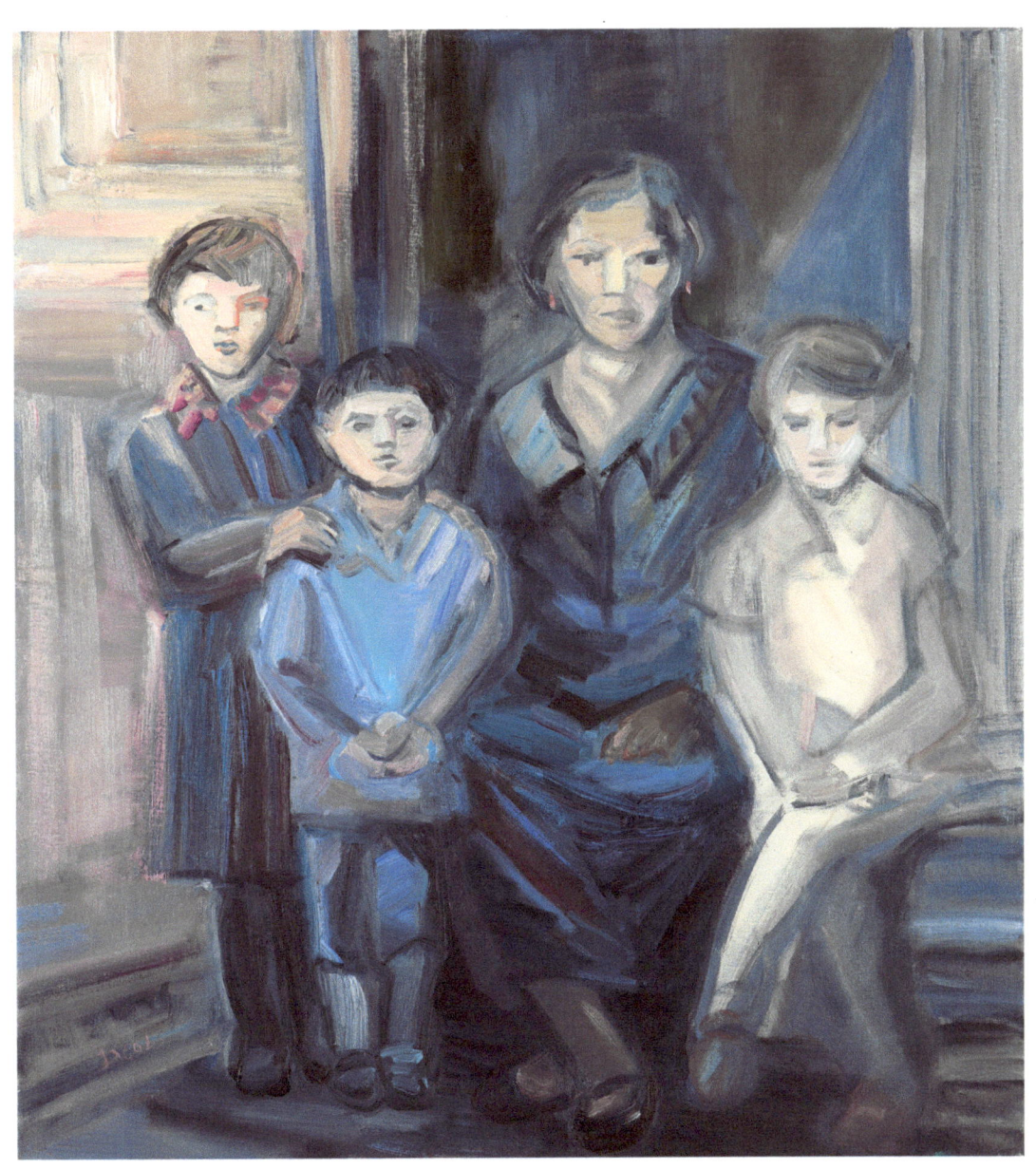

Huberman Family Portrait Color

Oil on linen, 34 x 30 inches, 2010

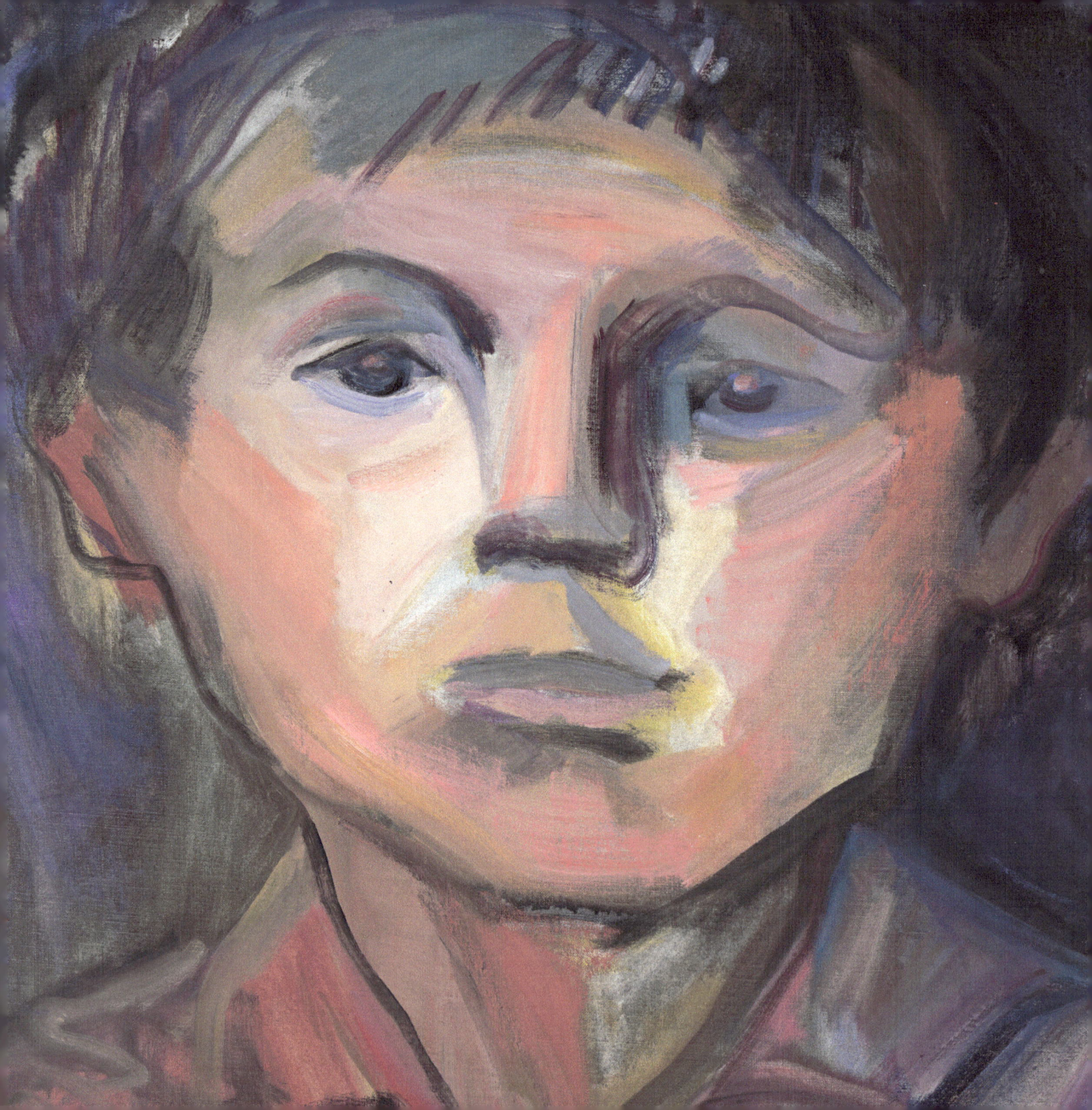

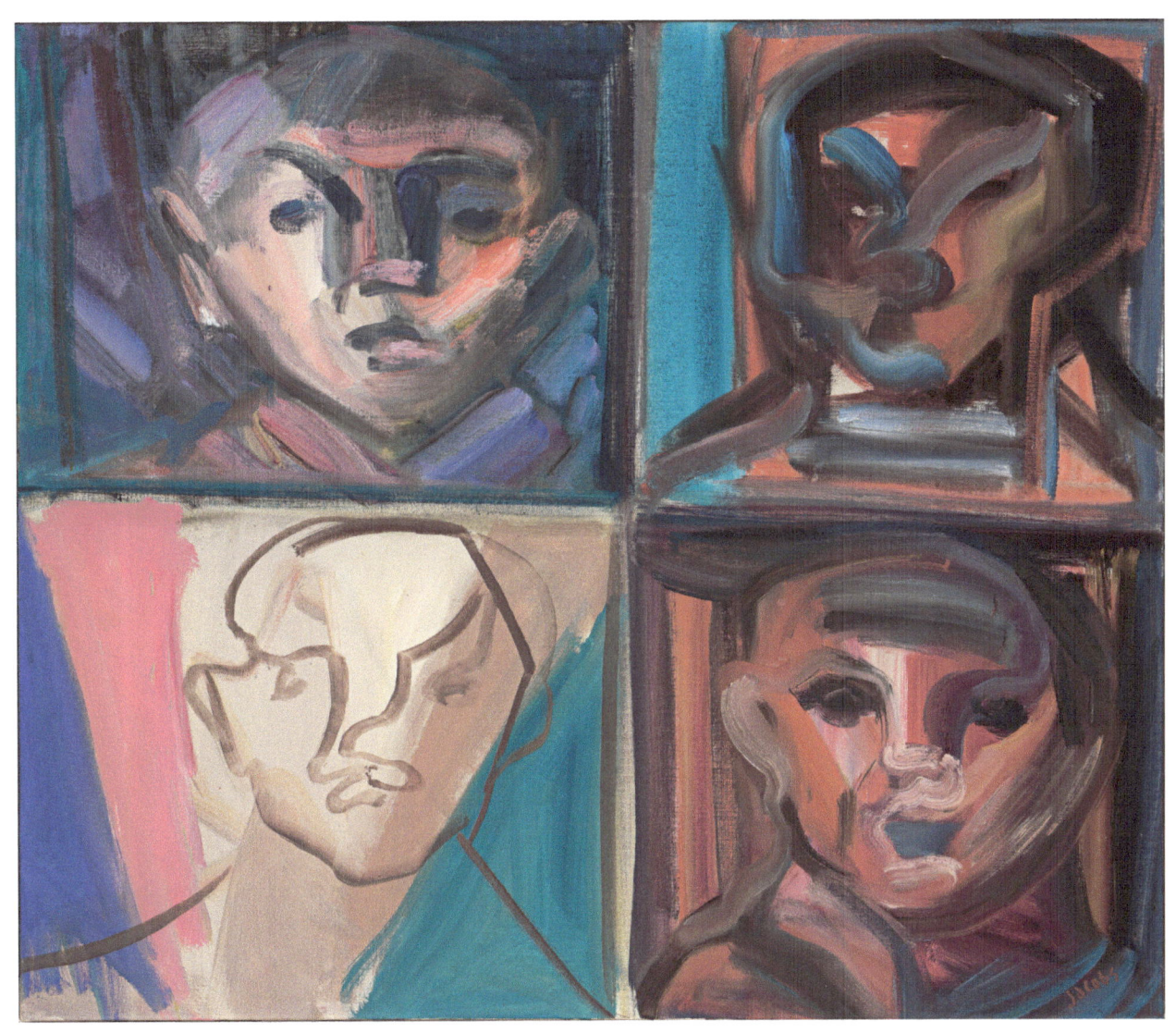

Kalman 13, oil on linen, 30 x 34 inches, 2007 (left)

Kalman Grid, oil on linen, 30 x 34 inches, 2007 (right)

INDEX OF COLOR PLATES

STILL LIFE

FIGURES

STAGES OF PAINTING SUNFLOWERS AT MONTCUQ

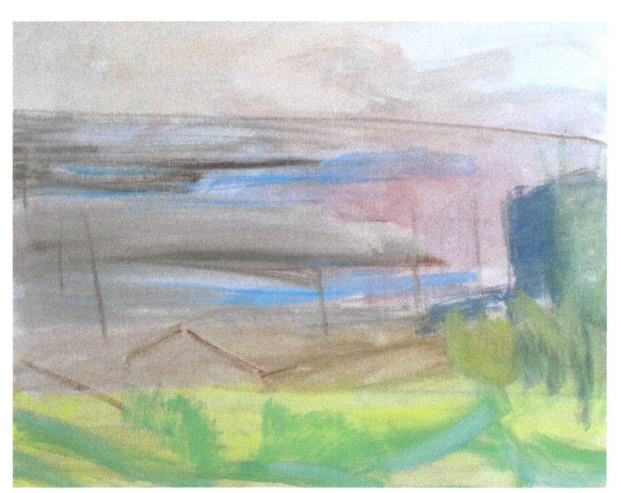 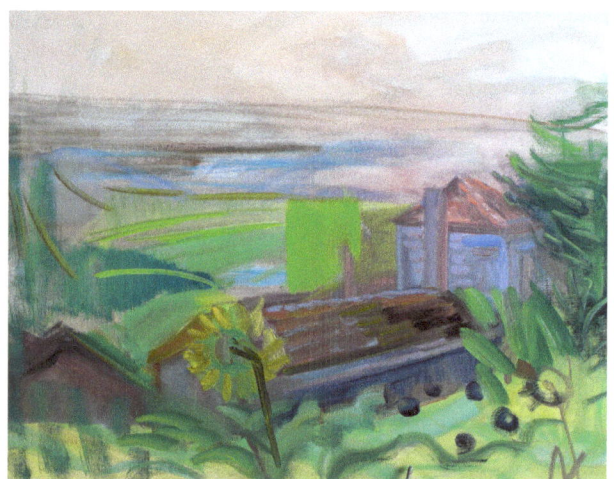

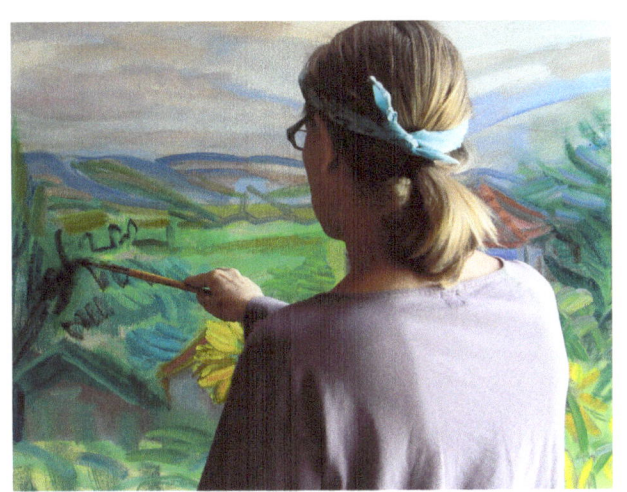
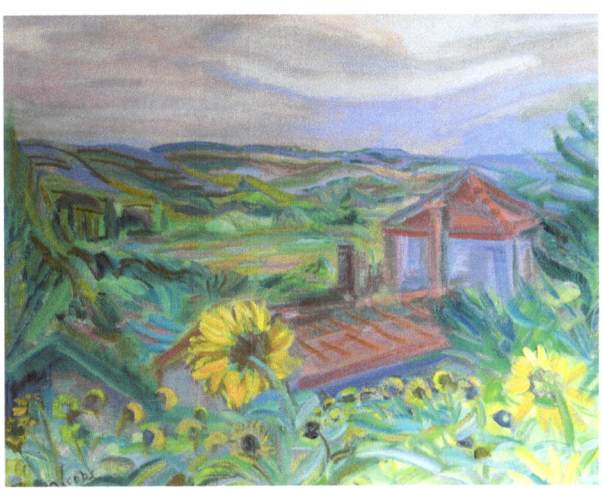

www.ingramcontent.com/pod-product-compliance
Lightning Source LLC
Chambersburg PA
CBHW050725180526
45159CB00003B/1134